D0681169

Cantonese Chinese
Phrase Book
&
Dictionary

Berlitz Publishing
New York   Munich   Singapore

Contacting the Editors
Every effort has been made to provide accurate information in this publication, but changes are inevitable. The publisher cannot be responsible for any resulting loss, inconvenience or injury. We would appreciate it if readers would call our attention to any errors or outdated information. We also welcome your suggestions; if you come across a relevant expression not in our phrase book, please contact us:
Berlitz Publishing, 193 Morris Avenue, Springfield, NJ 07081, USA. E-mail: comments@berlitzbooks.com

Second Printing: May 2010
Printed in China by CTPS

Publishing Director: Sheryl Olinsky Borg
Senior Editor/Project Manager: Lorraine Sova
Translation: Dr. Siu-lun Lee, Dr. Qiuxia Shao, Meihua Shi
Composition: Datagrafix, Inc.
Cover Design: Claudia Petrilli
Interior Design: Derrick Lim, Juergen Bartz
Production Manager: Elizabeth Gaynor
Cover Photo: © Fumio Okada/2003-2008 Oriental Touch Ltd.
Interior Photos: p. 14 © Studio Fourteen/Brand X Pictures/age fotostock; p. 19 © Jeff Banke, 2008. Used under license from Shutterstock, Inc.; p. 27 © Pixtal/age fotostock; p. 40 © Corbis/fotosearch.com; p. 51 © Purestock/Alamy; p. 56, 70 © Supri Suharjoto, 2008. Used under license from Shutterstock, Inc.; p. 60 © 2008 Jupiterimages Corporation; p. 79 © ImageDJ/Alamy; p. 83 © Netfalls/2003-2007 Shutterstock, Inc.; p. 93 © Boris Karpinski/Alamy; p. 96 © BananaStock Ltd.; p. 102 © Daniel Thistlethwaite/PictureQuest; p. 103 © Ulrike Hammerich, 2008. Used under license from Shutterstock, Inc.; p. 106 © Chee Choon Fat, 2008. Used under license from Shutterstock, Inc.; p. 110 © 2007 Jupiterimages Corporation; p. 117 © TongRo/Fotosearch.com; p. 126 © JLImages/Alamy; p. 133 © Jupiterimages/Brand X/Corbis; p. 135 © Stockbyte/Fotosearch.com; p. 139 © Corbis/2006 Jupiterimages Corporation; p. 141 © David McKee/2003-2007 Shutterstock, Inc.; p. 142, 146, 161 © 2007 Jupiterimages Corporation

Cor

Survival

3

Food

People

Fun

Special Needs

Resources

Dictionary

Pronunciation

The romanized pronunciation system widely used for Cantonese Chinese is the Yale romanization system. This system is used throughout the phrase book. Not all romanization letters or letter combinations are pronounced as they normally are in English. A guide to the pronunciation follows.

In addition to the Roman alphabet, Yale romanization also features tonal marks, which represent six Cantonese tones:

Tone	Mark	Description	Example	Chinese	Translation
1st	¯	high and level tone	sī	絲	silk
2nd	´	high, rising tone; starts medium in tone, then rises	sí	史	history
3rd		mid-level tone; flat, with no emphasis	si	試	try
4th	` h	low, falling tone; starts medium in tone and then falls sharp and strong	sìh*	時	time
5th	´ h	low, rising tone; starts low then rises to medium tone	síh*	市	city
6th	h	low and level tone	sih*	事	matter

*An "h" is placed after the vowel to indicate low tone.

Initial Consonants

Symbol	Approximate Pronunciation	Example	Pronunciation
gw	like qu in quiet	貴	gwai
kw	like k + w	裙	kwàhn
ch	between ch in church and ts in cats	叉	chā
j	between j in judge and ds in adds	炸	ja
m	like pronouncing m without opening the mouth	唔	m
ng	like ng in lying but further back in the mouth	我	ngóh

The letters b, d, f, g, h, k, l, m, n, p, s, t, w, y are pronounced generally as in English.

Finals

Symbol	Approximate Pronunciation	Example	Pronunciation
a	like a in father	沙	sā
e	like ai in fair	遮	jē
eu	like er in her	靴	hēu
i	like e in me	紙	jí
o	like o in dog	我	ngóh
u	like oo in cool	苦	fú
yu	like pronouncing you with lips pursed	書	syū

Symbol	Approximate Pronunciation	Example	Pronunciation
ai	like ei in Fahrenheit	雞	gāi
au	like ou in out	夠	gau
am	like um in umbrella	心	sām
an	like un in under	身	sān
ang	like un in uncle	生	sāng
ap	like up	十	sahp
at	like ut in utmost	實	saht
ak	like uck in luck	得	dāk
aai	like ai in aisle	街	gāai
aau	like ou in foul	教	gaau
aam	like am in Guam	三	sāam
aan	like aun in aunt	山	sāan
aang	like aun in aunt + g	行	hàahng
aap	like arp in harp	垃	laahp
aat	like art in cart	辣	laaht
aak	like ark in bark	肋	laahk
ei	like ei in eight	記	gei
eng	like e + ng	靚	leng
ek	like eck in deck	隻	jek
eui	like oi, pronunced with lips rounded	去	heui
eun	like en in enable, pronunced with lips rounded	信	seun
eut	like eu + t	出	chēut
eung	like eu + ng	香	hēung

Symbol	Approximate Pronunciation	Example	Pronunciation
euk	like eu + k	腳	geuk
iu	like il in until	笑	siu
im	like im in impolite	甜	tìhm
in	like in	天	tīn
ing	like ing in sing	星	sīng
ip	like ip in sip	涉	sip
it	like it in sit	洩	sit
ik	like ick in sick	識	sīk
ou	like ou in dough	好	hóu
oi	like oi in oil	開	hōi
on	like on	乾	gōn
ong	like on + g	江	gōng
ot	like ot in lot	渴	hot
ok	like auc in auction	各	gok
ui	like ui in cuisine	杯	būi
un	like oun in wound	半	bun
ut	like oo in wood + t	闊	fut
ung	like one in phone	中	jūng
uk	like oak	讀	duhk
yun	like yu + n	院	yún
yut	like yu + t	月	yuht

Cantonese is spoken in Hong Kong, Macau, Guangdong and Guangxi. There are approximately 64 million speakers of Cantonese in the world. Cantonese speakers can also be found in Malaysia, Vietnam, Singapore, Indonesia and among Chinese immigrants all over the world. Although Cantonese speakers read and write Mandarin Chinese, the Cantonese dialect is different in sentence structure, pronunciation and to a certain extent, grammar and vocabulary. This means that Cantonese speakers speak in one way (Cantonese dialect), but write in another way (Mandarin Chinese).

Written Chinese is not a combination of letters but ideograms. Each character represents a syllable of spoken Chinese; more than 80% of Chinese characters are actually compounds of two or more characters.

Chinese in written form can be traditional or simplified. Historically, traditional had been used in Hong Kong. Traditional Chinese has more strokes and is written vertically in columns from right to left or horizontally from left to right. Simplified Chinese has fewer strokes and is written horizontally from left to right. This phrase book features traditional Chinese.

How to Use This Book

These essential phrases can also be heard on the audio CD.

Sometimes you see two alternatives in italics, separated by a slash. Choose the one that's right for your situation.

Essential

I'm on *vacation [holiday]/business*.	我依家度假/出差。 ngóh yìh gā *douh ga/chēut chāai*
I'm going to…	我要去… ngóh yiu heui…
I'm staying at the… Hotel.	我住喺…酒店。 ngóh jyuh hái…jáu dim

You May See…

抵達 dái daaht	arrivals
離境 lèih gíng	departures
認領行李 yihng líhng hàhng léih	baggage claim

Finding Lodging

Can you recommend…?	你可唔可以介紹…? néih hó m hó yíh gaai siuh…
– a hotel	– 一間酒店 yāt gāan jáu dim
– a hostel	– 一間旅舍 yāt gāan léuih se
– a campsite	– 一個營地 yāt go yìhng deih

Words you may see are shown in *You May See* boxes.

Any of the words or phrases preceded by dashes can be plugged into the sentence above.

12

Cantonese Chinese phrases appear in red.

Read the simplified pronunciation as if it were English. For more on pronunciation, see page 7.

Relationships

How old are you?	你幾大年紀?	néih géi daaih nìhn géi
I'm…	我…	ngóh…

▶ For numbers, see page 157.

Are you married?	你結咗婚未?	né…
I'm…	我…	ngóh…

When different gender forms apply, the masculine form is followed by ♂; feminine by ♀.

– single/in a relationship	– 單身/有固定	dihng pàhng yáuh
– engaged/married	– 訂咗婚/結咗婚	dihng jó fān/git jó fān
– divorced/separated	– 離咗婚/分咗居	lèih jó fān/fān jó gēui
– widowed	– 老公♀/老婆♂過咗身	lóuh gūng ♀/lóuh pòh ♂gwo jó sān

The arrow indicates a cross reference where you'll find related phrases.

Information boxes contain relevant country, culture and language tips.

It is polite to address people with: 先生 **sin sāang** (Sir), 女士 **néuih sih** (Madam) or 小姐 **síu jé** (Miss).

You May Hear…

我講少少英文。	ngóh góng síu síu yīng màhn	I only speak a little English.
我唔識講英文。	ngóh m sīk góng yīng màhn	I don't speak English.

Expressions you may hear are shown in *You May Hear* boxes.

Color-coded side bars identify each section of the book.

▼ Survival

Arrival and Departure

Essential

I'm on *vacation* [holiday]/business.	我依家度假/出差。ngóh yìh gā *douh ga/chēut chāai*
I'm going to…	我要去… ngóh yiu heui…
I'm staying at the… Hotel.	我住喺…酒店。ngóh jyuh hái…jáu dim

You May Hear…

唔該護照。m gōi wuh jiu	Your passport, please.
你嚟嘅嘅目的係乜野？néih làih ge muhk dīk haih māt yéh	What's the purpose of your visit?
你住喺邊度？néih jyuh hái bīn douh	Where are you staying?
你留幾耐？néih làuh géi noih	How long are you staying?
邊個同你一齊嚟？bīn go tùhng néih yāt chàih làih	Who are you here with?

Passport Control and Customs

I'm just passing through.	我淨係過境。ngóh jihng haih gwo gíng
I'd like to declare…	我想申報… ngóh séung sān bou…
I have nothing to declare.	我唔使申報。ngóh m sái sān bou

U.S. and U.K. citizens must possess a valid passport and visa, issued by the Chinese authorities, to enter China. Tour groups may be issued group visas; the paperwork in this case would be handled by the travel agency.

U.S. and U.K. citizens need a valid passport only if their destination is Hong Kong alone.

Before you arrive in China, you will have to fill out a declaration form listing any valuables in your possession. When you leave China, you may be asked to show that you are taking with you the items listed, except for any items declared as gifts.

Contact your consulate for information on obtaining visas and for health requirements and travel advisories.

You May Hear...

使唔使申報？ sái m sái sān bou	Anything to declare?
呢件野你要畀稅。 nī gihn yéh néih yiu béi seui	You must pay duty on this.
唔該你打開呢個袋。 m gōi néih dá hōi nī go dói	Open this bag.

You May See...

海關 hói gwāan	customs
免稅物品 míhn seui maht bán	duty-free goods
申報物品 sān bou maht bán	goods to declare
不需要申報 bāt sēui yiu sān bou	nothing to declare
護照檢查 wuh jiu gím chàh	passport control
警員 gíng yùhn	police

Money and Banking

Essential

Where's…?	⋯喺邊度？ …hái bīn douh
– the ATM	– 自動提款機 jih duhng tàih fún gēi
– the bank	– 銀行 ngàhn hòhng
– the currency exchange office	– 貨幣兌換處 fo baih deui wuhn chyu
When does the bank *open/close*?	銀行幾時開門/閂門？ ngàhn hòhng géi sìh *hōi mùhn/sāan mùhn*
I'd like to change *dollars/pounds* into Hong Kong dollars.	我想將美金/英鎊換成港紙。 ngóh séung jēung *méih gām/yīng bóng* wuhn sìhng gong jí
I'd like to cash traveler's checks [cheques].	我想將旅行支票換成現金。 ngóh séung jēung léuih hàhng jī piu wuhn sìhng yihn gām

ATM, Bank and Currency Exchange

I'd like to *change money/get a cash advance*.	我想換錢/預支現金。 ngóh séung *wuhn chín/yuh jī yihn gām*
What's the exchange *rate/fee*?	外幣兌換率/費係幾多？ ngoih baih deui wuhn *léut/fai* haih géi dō
I think there's a mistake.	我覺得錯咗。 ngóh gok dāk cho jó
I lost my traveler's checks [cheques].	我唔見咗旅行支票。 ngóh m gin jó léuih hàhng jī piu
My credit card…	我嘅信用卡⋯ ngóh ge seun yuhng kāat…
– was lost	– 唔見咗 m gin jó

My credit card...	我嘅信用卡… ngóh ge seun yuhng kāat…
– was stolen	– 畀人偷咗 béi yàhn tāu jó
– doesn't work	– 唔用得 m yuhng dāk
The ATM ate my card.	自動取款機食咗我嘅信用卡。 jih duhng tàih fún gēi sihk jó ngóh ge seun yuhng kāat

i

Most major credit cards are accepted in Hong Kong and other major cities in China; however, they are accepted only at large shopping malls, stores and banks. A location that accepts credit card payment will display a credit card symbol in a visible place. Traveler's checks are accepted at most large banks in China, but you may have to pay a fee to cash them. Keep the receipt from the bank where your traveler's checks were issued; you may be asked to show the receipt when you have the checks cashed. You can change money at most banks. Some large stores provide this service as well. Cash is still the preferred payment method in China.

You May See...

插入信用卡 chāap yahp seun yuhng kāat	insert card here
取消 chéui sīu	cancel
清除 chīng chèuih	clear
進入 jeun yahp	enter
密碼 maht máh	PIN
取款 chéui fún	withdrawal
從支票帳戶取錢 chùhng jīpiu wu háu chéui chín	from checking [current account]
從儲蓄帳戶取錢 chùhng chyú chūk wuh háuh chéui chín	from savings
收據 sāu geui	receipt

i Chinese currency is 人民幣 **yàhn màhn baih** (Ren Min Bi, RMB), literally, "people's money", not tradable outside China. Currency used in Hong Kong is 港幣 **góng baih** (Hong Kong dollar). The monetary unit of Hong Kong dollars is the 蚊 **mān** (dollar), which is divided into 毫子 **hòuh jí** (ten cents). Bill denominations include 10, 20, 50, 100, 500, 1000 dollars; coins include 1, 2, 5, 10 dollars; 1 **hòuh jí,** 2 **hòuh jí,** 5 **hòuh jí.** One dollar is equal to 10 **hòuh jí.**

Transportation

Essential

How do I get to…?	我點去…? ngóh dím heui…
Where's…?	…喺邊度? …hái bīn douh
– the airport	– 機場 gēi chèuhng
– the train [railway] station	– 火車站 fó chē jaahm
– the bus station	– 巴士站 bā sí jaahm
– the subway [underground] station	– 地鐵站 deih tit jaahm
How far is…?	…有幾遠? …yáuh géi yúhn
Where do I buy a ticket?	我喺邊度買飛? ngóh hái bīn douh máaih fēi
A *one-way/round-trip [return]* ticket to…	一張去…嘅單程/雙程飛 yāt jēung heui…ge *dāan chìhng/sēung chìhng* fēi
How much?	幾多錢? géi dō chín
Which…?	邊…? bīn…
– gate	– 個閘口 go jaahp háu
– line	– 條線 tìuh sin
– platform	– 個月台 go yuht tòih
Where can I get a taxi?	我喺邊度可以搵到的士? ngóh hái bīn douh hó yíh wándóu dīk sí
Take me to this address.	將我送到呢個地址。 jēung ngóh sung dou nīgo deih jí
Can I have a map?	我可唔可以買一張地圖? ngóh hó m hó yíh máaih yāt jēung deih tòuh

Ticketing

When's…to Tsimshatsui?	去尖沙咀嘅⋯⋯係乜野時間？ heui jīm sā jéui ge…haih māt yéh sìh gaan
– the (first) bus	–（第一班）巴士 (daih yāt bāan) bā sí
– the (next) flight	–（下一班）飛機 (hah yāt bāan) fēi gēi
– the (last) train	–（最後一班）火車 (jeui hauh yāt bāan) fó chē
Where do I buy a ticket?	我喺邊度買飛？ ngóh hái bīn douh máaih fēi
One ticket/two tickets, please.	唔該你畀一張/兩張飛我。 m gōi néih béi yāt jēung/léuhng jēung fēi ngóh
For *today/tomorrow*.	要今日/聽日嘅。 yiu *gām yaht/tīng yaht* ge

▶ For days, see page 161.

▶ For time, see page 160.

…ticket.	一張⋯⋯飛。 yāt jēung…fēi
– A one-way	– 單程 dāan chìhng
– A round-trip [return]	– 雙程 sēung chìhng
– A first class	– 頭等艙 tàuh dáng chōng
– A business class	– 商務艙 sēung mouh chōng
– An economy class	– 經濟艙 gīng jai chōng
How much?	幾多錢？ géi dō chín
Is there…discount?	⋯⋯有冇折？ …yáuh móuh jit
– a child	– 細蚊仔 sai mān jái
– a student	– 學生 hohk sāang
– a senior citizen	– 老人 lóuh yàhn
– a tourist	– 遊客 yàuh haak
I have an e-ticket.	我有一張電子飛。 ngóh yáuh yāt jēung dihn jí fēi
Can I buy a ticket on the *bus/train*?	我可唔可以喺巴士/火車上面買飛票？ ngóh hó m hó yíh hái *bā sí/fó chē* seuhng mihn máaih fēi

How long is this ticket valid?	呢張飛有效時間係幾耐？ nī jēung fēi yáuh haauh sìh gaan haih géi noih
Can I return on the same ticket?	我可唔可以用同一張飛返嚟？ ngóh hó m hó yíh yuhng tùhng yāt jēung fēi fāan làih
I'd like to…my reservation.	我想…我定嘅位。 ngóh séung…ngóh dehng ge wái
– cancel	– 取消 chéui sīu
– change	– 改變 gói bin
– confirm	– 確認 kok yihng

Plane

Getting to the Airport

How much is a taxi to the airport?	去機場坐的士要幾多錢？ heui gēi chèuhng chóh dīk sí yiu géi dō chín
To…Airport, please.	唔該你帶我去…機場。 m gōi néih daai ngóh heui… gēi chèuhng
My airline is…	我嘅航空公司係… ngóh ge hòhng hūng gūng sī haih…
My flight leaves at…	我嘅航班…起飛 ngóh ge hòhng bāan…héi fēi
I'm in a rush.	我依家趕時間。 ngóh yìh gā gón sìh gaan

▶ For time, see page 160.

| Can you take an alternate route? | 你可唔可以行第二條路？ néih hó m hó yíh hàahng daih yih tìuh louh |
| Can you drive *faster/slower*? | 你可唔可以揸快/慢啲？ néih hó m hó yíh jā *faai/maahn dī* |

You May Hear…

| 你坐邊間航空公司嘅班機？ néih chóh bīn gāan hòhng hūng gūng sī ge bāan gēi | What airline are you flying? |
| 國內定係國際航班？ gwok noih dihng haih gwok jai hòhng bāan | Domestic or international? |

邊一個候機大堂？ bīn yāt go hauh gēi daaih tòhng   **What terminal?**

i Many U.S. and U.K. airlines have frequent flights to and from Hong Kong and other major cities in China. The procedure for departure and arrivals are similar to those at an airport in the U.S. and U.K. Duty-free stores as well as transportation from the airport to the downtown area are available at most international Chinese airports.

If you plan on traveling throughout China, it is a good idea to make travel arrangements in advance. There are a few main tourist information offices that can help you to book tickets, hotels and flights: China International Travel Service (CITS), China Travel Service (CTS) and China Youth Travel Sevice (CYTS). Visit their websites for more information. Keep in mind that reservations often need to be made well in advance.

▶For useful websites, see page 165.

You May See...

抵達 dái daaht	arrivals
離境 lèih gíng	departures
認領行李 yihng líhng hàhng léih	baggage claim
安全 ngōn chyùhn	security
國內航班 gwok noih hòhng bāan	domestic flights
國際航班 gwok jai hòhng bāan	international flights
辦理登機手續 baahn léih dāng gēi sáu juhk	check-in
辦理電子登機手續 baahn léih dihn jí dāng gēi sáu juhk	e-ticket check-in
登機口 dāng gēi háu	departure gates

Check-in and Boarding

Where's check-in?	喺邊度辦理登機手續？ hái bīn douh baahn léih dāng gēi sáu juhk
My name is…	我叫… ngóh giu…
I'm going to…	我要去… ngóh yiu heui…
I have…	我有… ngóh yáuh…
– one suitcase	– 一個行李箱 yāt go hàhng léih sēung
– two suitcases	– 兩個行李箱 léuhng go hāhng léih sēung
– one carry-on [piece of hand luggage]	– 一件隨身行李 yāt gihn chèuih sān hàhng léih
How much luggage is allowed?	可以帶幾件行李？ hó yíh daai géi gihn hàhng léih
Which *terminal/gate*?	邊個候機大堂/登機口？ bīngo *hauh gēi daaih tòhng/dāng gēi háu*
I'd like *a window/ an aisle* seat.	我想要窗口/路口位。 ngóh séung yiu *chēung háu/louh háu* wái
When do we *leave/ arrive*?	我哋幾點離開/到？ ngóh deih géi dím *lèih hōi/dou*
Is the flight delayed?	飛機係唔係遲咗？ Fēi gēi haih m haih chìh jó
How late?	有幾遲？ yáuh géi chìh

嗰件隨身行李太大。gó gihn chèuih sān hàhng léih taai daaih		That's too large for a carry-on [to carry on board].
唔該除鞋。m gōi chèuih hàaih		Take off your shoes.
依家…登機。yìhgā…dāng gēi		Now boarding…

Luggage

Where *is/are*…?	…喺邊度？ …hái bīn douh
– the luggage carts [trolleys]	– 手推車 sáu tēui chē
– the luggage lockers	– 行李暫存箱 hàhng léih jaahm chyùhn sēung
– the baggage claim	– 認領行李 yihng líhng hàhng léih
My luggage has been *lost/stolen*.	我嘅行李唔見咗/畀人偷咗。ngóh ge hàhng léih *m gin jó/béi yàhn tāu jó*
My suitcase is damaged.	我嘅手提箱畀人整壞咗。ngóh ge sáu tàih sēung béi yàhn jíng waaih jó

Finding Your Way

Where *is/are*…?	…喺邊度？ …hái bīn douh
– the currency exchange	– 換錢 wuhn chín
– the car rental [hire]	– 租車 jōu chē
– the exit	– 出口 chēut háu
– the taxis	– 的士 dīk sí
Is there…to Guangzhou?	有冇去廣州嘅…？ yáuh móuh heui gwóng jāu ge…
– a bus	– 巴士 bā sí
– a train	– 火車 fó chē
– a subway [metro]	– 地鐵 deih tit

▶ For directions, see page 35.

Train

Where's the train [railway] station?	火車站喺邊度？ fó chē jaahm hái bīn douh
How far is…?	…有幾遠？ …yáuh géi yúhn
Where *is/are*…?	…喺邊度？ …hái bīn douh
– the ticket office	– 售票處 sauh piu chyu
– the information desk	– 訊問處 sēun mahn chyu
– the luggage lockers	– 行李暫存箱 hàhng léih jaahm chyùhn sēung
– the platforms	– 月台 yuht tòih

▶ For directions, see page 35.

▶ For ticketing, see page 21.

You May See...

月台 yuht tòih	platforms
信息 seuhn sīk	information
預定 yuh dehng	reservations
候車室 hauh chē sāt	waiting room
抵達 dái daaht	arrivals
離開 lèih hōi	departures

Questions

Can I have a schedule [timetable]?	畀一張時間表我好唔好？ béi yāt jēung sìh gaan bíu ngóh hóu m hóu
Is it a direct train?	係唔係直到？ haih m haih jihk dou
Do I have to change trains?	我使唔使轉車？ ngóh sái m sái jyun chē

| How long is the trip? | 要幾耐時間？ | yiu géi noih sìh gaan |
| Is the train on time? | 火車準唔準時？ | fó chē jéun m jéun sìh |

China has a vast rail network and you can travel by train to almost every Chinese city and town. There are different types of train services available: 快車 **faai chē** (express), 慢車 **maahn chē** (regular) and 直達 **jihk daaht** (non-stop). There are five classes of seats: hard seat, soft seat, hard sleeper, soft sleeper and standing. Buy a ticket at the train station or from one of the ticket offices located throughout the major cities. Before boarding, have your ticket validated by an attendant at the station. There may be machines to validate your tickets in the larger cities.

In addition to extensive rail service, Hong Kong, Shenzhen and Guangzhou also have subway systems. Buy your ticket at the subway station from a vending machine and validate it at the ticket machine.

Departures

Which track [platform] to…?	邊個月台去…？ bīn go yuht tòih heui…
Is this the *track [platform]/train* to…?	呢個係唔係去…嘅月台/火車？ nī go haih m haih heui…ge *yuht tòih/fó chē*
Where is track [platform]…?	…月台喺邊度？ …yuht tòih hái bīn douh
Where do I change for…?	我點樣轉車去…？ ngóh dím yéung jyun chē heui…

Boarding

Can I *sit here/open the window?*	我可唔可以坐喺呢度/打開窗？ ngóh hó m hó yíh *chóh hái nī douh/dá hōi chēung*
That's my seat.	嗰個係我嘅位。 gó go haih ngóh ge wái
Here's my reservation.	我訂咗呢個位。 ngóh dehng jó nī go wái

You May Hear…

請大家上車！ chéng daaih gā séuhng chē	All aboard!
唔該車飛。 m gōi chē fēi	Tickets, please.
你要喺九龍堂轉車。 néih yiu hái gáu lùhng tòhng jyun chē	You have to change at Kowloon Tong.
下一站係尖沙咀。 hah yāt jaahm haih jīm sā jéui	Next stop, Tsim Sha Tsui.

Bus

Where's the bus station?	車站喺邊度？ chē jaahm hái bīn douh
How far is it?	有幾遠？ yáuh géi yúhn

How do I get to…?	我點樣去…?	ngóh dím yéung heui…
Is this the bus to…?	呢架係唔係去…嘅巴士?	nī ga haih m haih heui…ge bā sí
Can you tell me when to get off?	你可唔可以話畀我知幾時落車?	néih hó m hó yíh wah béi ngóh jī géi sìh lohk chē
Do I have to change buses?	我使唔使轉巴士?	ngóh sái m sái jyun bā sí
How many stops to…?	到…有幾多個站?	dou…yáuh géi dō go jaahm
Stop here, please!	唔該喺呢度停車!	m gōi hái nī douh tìhng chē

▶For ticketing, see page 21.

---

i

There are three kinds of bus systems in China: public buses for city transportation, tourist buses for sightseeing and long-distance buses for travel outside of town. Most buses run from 6 a.m. to 11 p.m. In major cities, you can purchase a monthly discounted pass for public buses. Tourist buses, which are available in major cities, may offer flexible fares (especially for groups) so be sure to negotiate with the driver. Long-distance buses in China offer service to practically every small town, including those in remote regions not accessible by train or plane. There is a bus station in almost every town, big and small, where you can find information regarding the bus schedule, fares, routes, etc. For public and long-distance buses, buy your ticket at the bus station and have it validated by an attendant before boarding. In Hong Kong, you can also pay the fare when you get on the bus or you can buy a prepaid card, 八達通 **baat daaht tūng** (also known as an octopus card), at train and subway stations; these "octopus" cards can be used on all types of public transportation throughout the city.

巴士站 bā sí jaahm	bus stop
上車/落車 séuhng chē/lohk chē	enter/exit

Subway [Underground]

Where's the subway [underground] station?	地鐵站喺邊度？ deih tit jaahm hái bīn douh
A map, please.	唔該畀一張地圖我。 m gōi béi yāt jēung deih tòuh ngóh
Which line for...?	邊條線去…？ bīn tìuh sin heui...
Which direction?	邊個方向？ bīn go fōng heung
Do I have to transfer [change]?	我使唔使轉地鐵？ ngóh sái m sái jyun deih tit
Is this the subway [metro] to...?	呢架地鐵去唔去…？ nī ga deih tit heui m heui...
How many stops to...?	到…有幾多個站？ dou...yáuh géi dō go jaahm
Where are we?	我哋喺邊度？ ngóh deih hái bīn douh

▶ For ticketing, see page 21.

Major cities in China, including Hong Kong, Guangzhou and Shenzhen, have subway systems. Purchase one-trip tickets and discounted monthly passes at subway stations; some cities may also offer daily and/or weekend tickets. Request operation times, routes, fares and other subway information from the ticket booth attendant. At some stations, you simply pay and enter; at others, you buy a ticket at the booth and have the ticket validated by an attendant before boarding. There may be validation machines in large cities. Maps are available at the ticket booth, usually for a fee.

Boat and Ferry

When is the ferry to...?

去…嘅渡輪係乜野時間？ heui...ge douh lèuhn haih māt yéh sìh gaan

Where are the life jackets?

救生衣喺邊度？ gau sāng yī hái bīn douh

▶ For ticketing, see page 21.

You May See...

救生船 gau sāng syùhn   life boat

救生衣 gau sāng yī   life jacket

There is regular ferry and boat service between large coastal cities of China as well as along rivers, particularly the Chang Jiang (Yangzi) and Zhu Jiang (Pearl) but not the Huang He (Yellow). Some islands in Guangdong are accessible by ferry. Check with a travel agent or the local ferry terminal for schedules, routes and fares.

There is regular ferry service between Hong Kong island and Kowloon. The Hong Kong ferry is a main tourist attraction because of the renowned night scenery, which includes views of the coastal area of Hong Kong island and Kowloon pennisula. There is also regular ferry service between Hong Kong island and nearby outlying islands.

Bicycle and Motorcycle

I'd like to rent [hire] a *bicycle/motorcycle*.	我想租一架單車/一架電單車。ngóh séung jōu *yāt ga dāan chē/yāt ga dihn dāan chē*
How much per *day/week*?	一日/個星期幾多錢? *yāt yaht/go sīng kèih* géi dō chín
Can I have a *helmet/lock*?	我可唔可以買一個頭盔/一把鎖? ngóh hó m hó yíh máaih yāt go *tòuh kwāi/yāt bá só*

> *i*
>
> Cycling is a popular method of transportation throughout China. Bicycles can be rented in many Chinese towns, either at hotels or bicycle shops. To avoid parking fines and to minimize the risk of having the bicycle stolen, park the bicycle at guarded parking spaces for a small fee.
>
> In Hong Kong, cycling is mainly for recreational purposes. Since the traffic in Hong Kong is extremely busy, it is dangerous to ride bicycles within congested city areas.

Taxi

Where can I get a taxi?	我喺邊度可以叫的士? ngóh hái bīndouh hó yíh giu dīk sí
Do you have the number for a taxi?	你有冇的士公司電話? néih yáuh móuh dīk sí gūng sī dihn wá
I'd like a taxi *now/for tomorrow* at…	我宜家/聽日喺…想叫的士。ngóh *yìh gā/tīng yaht hái*…séung giu dīk sí
Pick me up at…	喺…接我。 hái…jip ngóh
I'm going to…	我要去… ngóh yiu heui…
– this address	– 呢個地址 nī go deih jí
– the airport	– 機場 gēi chèuhng
– the train [railway] station	– 火車站 fó chē jaahm

I'm late.	我遲咗。 ngóh chìh jó
Can you drive *faster/slower*?	你可唔可以開快/慢啲？ néih hó m hó yíh hōi *faai/maahn dī*
Stop/Wait here.	喺呢度停車/等我。 hái nī douh *tìhng chē/dáng ngóh*
How much?	幾多錢？ géi dō chín
You said it would cost…	你講過要… néih góng gwo yiu…
Can I have a receipt?	我可唔可以要收據？ ngóh hó m hó yíh yiu sāu geui
Keep the change.	唔使找喇。 m sái jáau la

You May Hear...

去邊度？ heui bīn douh	Where to?
地址係乜野？ deih jí haih māt yéh	What's the address?
有夜間/機場附加費。 yáuh *yeh gāan/gēi chèuhng* fuh ga fai	There's a *nighttime/ airport* surcharge.

i

Taxi service in Hong Kong and most other main cities in China is usually meter-based; in smaller towns or in the countryside, you may need to negotiate a flat fee with the driver. Hail a taxi on the street by raising your arm or grab a taxi at taxi stands, located throughout major cities and recognizable by a TAXI sign. There is usually no surcharge for luggage, but a nighttime surcharge may apply. Tipping the taxi driver is not a norm in China, but will be happily accepted.

Car Rental [Hire]

Where's the car rental [hire]?	喺邊度租車? hái bīn douh jōu chē
I'd like…	我想要… ngóh séung yiu…
– a *cheap/small* car	– 一架平啲/細啲嘅車 yāt ga *pèhng dī/sai dī* ge chē
– an automatic/ a manual	– 手波/自動波 sáu bō/jih duhng bō
– air conditioning	– 冷氣 láahng hei
– a car seat	– 兒童安全座位 yìh túhng ngō chyùhn joh wái
How much…?	…幾多錢? …géi dō chín
– per *day/week*	– 每日/個星期 múih *yaht/go sīng kèih*
– per kilometer	– 每公里 múih gūng léih
– for unlimited mileage	– 不限里程 bāt haahn léih chìhng
– with insurance	– 有保險 yáuh bóu hím
Are there any discounts?	有冇折? yáuh móuh jit

You May Hear…

你有冇國際車牌? néih yáuh móuh gwokjai chē pàaih	Do you have an international driver's license?
唔該你出示你嘅護照。 m gōi néih chēut sih néih ge wuhtjiu	Your passport, please.
你想唔想買保險? néih séung m séung máaih bóu hím	Do you want insurance?
我需要按金。 ngóh sēui yiu ngon gām	I'll need a deposit.
喺呢度簽你嘅名。 hái nī douh chīm néih ge méng	Sign here.

i Car rental agencies are available only in major cities for driving within the city limits. You can, however, hire a driver for a few hours, a day or longer at a rate that you can negotiate. Talk to your hotel concierge about safe rental options.

Gas [Petrol] Station

Where's the gas [petrol] station?	油站喺邊度？	yàuh jaahm hái bīn douh
Fill it up.	唔該入滿。	m gōi yahp múhn
I'll pay *in cash/by credit card.*	我用現金/信用卡畀錢。	ngóh yuhng *yihn gām/seun yuhng kāat* béi chín

▶ For numbers, see page 157.

You May See...

汽油 hei yàuh	gas [petrol]
有鉛 yáuh yùhn	leaded
無鉛 mòuh yùhn	unleaded
普通 póu tūng	regular
超級 chīu kāp	super
優質 yāu jāt	premium
柴油 chàaih yàuh	diesel
自助服務 jih joh fuhk mouh	self-service
全面服務 chyùhn mihn fuhk mouh	full-service

Asking Directions

Is this the way to...?	呢度係唔係去…嘅路？	nī douh haih m haih heui...ge louh
How far is it to...?	去…有幾遠？	heui...yáuh géi yúhn

35

Where's...?	…喺邊度？ …hái bīn douh
– ...Street	– …街 …gāai
– this address	– 呢個地址 nī go deih jí
– the highway [motorway]	– 高速公路 gōu chūk gūng louh
Can you show me on the map?	你可唔可以喺地圖上面指畀我睇？ néih hó m hó yíh hái deih tòuh seuhng mihn jí béi ngóh tái
I'm lost.	我盪失路。 ngóh dohng sāt louh

You May Hear...

一直向前 yāt jihk heung chìhn	straight ahead
左邊 jó bīn	left
右邊 yauh bī	right
喺/轉過街角 hái/jyun gwo gāai gok	on/around the corner
對面 deui mihn	opposite
後面 hauh mihn	behind
旁邊 pòhng bīn	next to
後 hauh	after
北/南 bāk/nàahm	north/south
東/西 dūng/sāi	east/west
喺交通燈嗰度 hái gāau tūng dāng gó douh	at the traffic light
喺十字路口 hái sahp jih louh háu	at the intersection

You May See...

| 停 tìhng | stop |
| 讓 yeuhng | yield [give way] |

不准駛入 bāt jéun sái yahp	do not enter
禁區 gam kēui	restricted area
進入 jeun yahp	enter
轉左 jyun jó	turn left
轉右 jyun yauh	turn right
停車場 tìhng chē chèuhng	parking lot [car park]
入口 yahp háu	entrance
出口 chēut háu	exit
行人路 hàahng yàhn louh	pedestrian road

Parking

Can I park here?	我可唔可以停喺呢度？ ngóh hó m hó yíh tìhng hái nī douh
Where's…?	…喺邊度？ …hái bīn douh
– the parking garage	– 車房 chē fòhng
– the parking lot [car park]	– 停車場 tìhng chē chèuhng
– the parking meter	– 停車計時器 tìhng chē gai sìh hei
How much…?	幾多錢…？ géi dō chín…
– per hour	– 每個鐘頭 múih go jūng tàuh
– per day	– 每日 múih yaht
– overnight	– 通宵 tūng sīu

Breakdown and Repairs

My car *broke down/ won't start.*	我嘅車壞咗/唔行得。ngóh ge chē *waaih jó/m hàahng dāk*
Can you fix it?	你可唔可以整好？ néih hó m hó yíh jíng hóu

37

| When will it be ready? | 幾時可以整好? géi sìh hó yíh jíng hóu |
| How much? | 幾多錢? géi dō chín |

Accidents

| There was an accident. | 有意外。yáuh yi ngoih |
| Call *an ambulance/ the police*. | 打電話叫一架救護車/警察。dá dihn wá giu yāt ga *gau wuh chē/gíng chaat* |

Accommodations

Essential

Can you recommend a hotel?	你可唔可以推薦一間酒店? néih hó m hó yíh tēui jin yāt gāan jáu dim
I have a reservation.	我定咗房。ngóh dehng jó fóng
My name is…	我嘅名係… ngóh ge méng haih…
Do you have a room…?	有冇…嘅房間? yáuh móuh…ge fòhnggāan
– for *one/two*	– 一/兩個人 *yāt/léuhng* go yàhn
– with a bathroom	– 有沖涼房 yáuh chūng lèuhng fóng
– with air conditioning	– 有冷氣 yáuh láahng hei
For…	住… jyuh…
– tonight	– 今晚 gām máahn
– two nights	– 兩晚 léuhng máahn
– one week	– 一個星期 yāt go sīng kèih
How much?	幾多錢? géi dō chín
Is there anything cheaper?	有冇平啲嘅? yáuh móuh pèhng dī ge

When's check-out?	幾點退房？géi dím teui fóng
Can I leave these in the safe?	我可唔可以將呢啲野留喺保險箱？ngóh hó m hó yíh jēung nī dī yéh láuh hái bóu hím sēung
Can I leave my bag?	我可唔可以將呢個袋留低？ngóh hó m hó yíh jēung nī go dói làuh dāi
I'll pay *in cash/by credit card*.	我用現金/信用卡畀錢。ngóh yuhng *yihn gām*/*seun yuhng kāat* béi chín
Can I have my receipt?	可唔可以畀收據我？hó m hó yíh béi sāu geui ngóh

Hotels, 酒店 **jáu dim**, in China range from budget to luxury. Many quality hotels belong to international hotel chains with service and prices to match. Larger hotels may feature an English-speaking service attendant who holds room keys; handles laundry; sells cigarettes, snacks, drinks and postcards and offers general assistance. If available, postal, phone and foreign exchange services are usually located on the first floor.

In general, hotels are ranked from three to five stars; the majority of hotels charge a 10–15% service fee. Be sure to reserve accommodations in advance, especially if you plan on visiting China during the main tourist seasons: May, September and October.

Worth mentioning are the famous, well-preserved hotels dating from colonial times: Peninsula Hotel Hong Kong, Island Shang-ri-la Hong Kong, Garden Hotel Guangzhou and White Swan Guangzhou. Reservations for these must be made well in advance.

Finding Lodging

Can you recommend…?	你可唔可以介紹…？néih hó m hó yíh gaai siuh…
– a hotel	– 一間酒店 yāt gāan jáu dim

Can you recommend…?	你可唔可以介紹…? néih hó m hó yíh gaai siuh…
– a hostel	– 一間旅舍 yāt gāan léuih se
– a campsite	– 一個營地 yāt go yìhng deih
– a bed and breakfast	– 一間有早餐嘅酒店 yāt gāan yáuh jóu chāan ge jáu dim
What is it near?	呢度離邊度近? nī douh lèih bīn douh káhn
How do I get there?	我點去嗰度呢? ngóh dím heui gó douh nē

At the Hotel ─────────

I have a reservation.	我訂咗。 ngóh dehng jó
My name is…	我嘅名係… ngóh ge méng haih…
Do you have a room…?	有冇…嘅房? yáuh móuh…ge fóng
– with a bathroom	– 有沖涼房 yáuh chūng lèuhng fóng
– with air conditioning	– 有冷氣 yáuh láahng hei
– that's *smoking/ non-smoking*	– 嗰間係吸煙/非吸煙房 gó gāan haih *kāp yīn/fēi kāp yīn* fóng

For…	住… jyuh…
– tonight	– 今晚 gām máahn
– two nights	– 兩晚 léuhng máahn
– a week	– 一個星期 yāt go sīng kèih

▶ For numbers, see page 157.

Do you have…?	你有冇…? néih yáuh móuh…
– a computer	– 電腦 dihn nouh
– an elevator [a lift]	– 電梯 dihn tāi
– (wireless) internet service	–（無線）互聯網服務 (mòuh sin) wuh lyùhn móhng fuhk mouh
– room service	– 客房送餐服務 haak fóng sung chāan fuhk mouh
– a TV	– 電視機 dihn sih gēi
– a pool	– 游泳池 yàuh wihng chìh
– a gym	– 健身房 gihn sān fóng
I need…	我需要… ngóh sēui yiu…
– an extra bed	– 加床 gā chòhng
– a cot	– 一張BB床 yāt jēung bìh bī chòhng
– a crib	– 一個搖籃 yāt go yìuh láam

You May Hear…

唔該你出示你嘅護照/信用卡。m gōi néih chēut sih néih ge *wuh jiu/seun yuhng kāat*	Your *passport/credit card*, please.
填好呢份表格。tìhn hóu nī fahn bíu gaak	Fill out this form.
喺呢度簽名。hái nī douh chīm méng	Sign here.

Price

How much per *night/ week*?	每晚/星期幾多錢? múih *máahn/sīng kèih* géi dō chín

41

Does that include *breakfast/sales tax [VAT]*?	包唔包早餐/銷售稅？bāau m bāau *jóu chāan/sīu sauh seui*
Are there any discounts?	有冇折？yáuh móuh jit

Decisions

Can I see the room?	我可唔可以睇吓間房？ngóh hó m hó yíh tái háh gāan fóng
I'd like…room.	我想要一間…嘅房。ngóh séung yiu yāt gāan…ge fóng
– a better	– 好啲 hóu dī
– a bigger	– 大啲 daaih dī
– a cheaper	– 平啲 pèhng dī
– a quieter	– 靜啲 jihng dī
I'll take it.	我要呢間房。ngóh yiu nī gāan fóng
No, I won't take it.	唔要，我唔要呢間房。m yiu ngóh m yiu nī gāan fóng

Questions

Where's…?	…喺邊度？…hái bīn douh
– the bar	– 酒吧 jáu bā
– the bathroom [toilet]	– 浴室 yuhk sāt
– the elevator [lift]	– 電梯 dihn tāi
Can I have…?	我可唔可以要…？ngóh hó m hó yíh yiu…
– a blanket	– 一張毯 yāt jēung jīn
– an iron	– 一個熨斗 yāt go tong dáu
– the *room key/key card*	– 房間鎖匙/鎖匙卡 fòhng gāan *só sìh/só sih kāat*
– a pillow	– 一個枕頭 yāt go jám tàuh
– soap	– 一舊番鹼 yāt gauh fāan gáan

– toilet paper	– 廁紙 chi jí
– a towel	– 一條毛巾 yāt tìuh mòuh gān
Do you have an adapter for this?	你有冇呢個火牛？ néih yáuh móuh nī go fó ngàuh
How do I turn on the lights?	我點樣開燈？ ngóh dím yéung hōi dāng
Can you wake me at…?	你可唔可以…叫醒我？ néih hó m hó yíh…giu séng ngóh

▶ For time, see page 160.

Can I leave these in the safe?	我可唔可以將呢啲野留喺保險箱？ ngóh hó m hó yíh jēung nī dī yéh làuh hái bóu hím sēung
Is there *mail [post]/ a message* for me?	有冇郵件/留言畀我？ yáuh móuh *yàuh gín/làuh yìhn* béi ngóh
What time do you lock up?	幾點鎖門？ géi dím só mùhn

The voltage used in China is 220. You will need an adapter for any appliances and electronics brought into the country.

You May See...

推/拉 tēui/lāai	push/pull
沖涼房 chūng lèuhng fóng	restroom [toilet]
花灑 fā sá	shower
電梯 dihn tāi	elevator [lift]
樓梯 làuh tāi	stairs
洗衣 sái yī	laundry
請勿打擾 chíng maht dá yíu	do not disturb
防火門 fòhng fó mùhn	fire door

(緊急)出口 (gán gáp) chēut háu		(emergency) exit
電話叫醒 dihn wá giu séng		wake-up call

Problems

There's a problem.	有問題。yáuh mahn tàih
I lost *my key/key card*.	我唔見咗鎖匙/鎖匙卡。ngóh m gin jó *só sìh/só sih kāat*
There's no *hot water/toilet paper*.	冇熱水/廁紙。móuh *yiht séui/chi jí*
The room is dirty.	房好烏糟。fóng hóu wū jōu
There are bugs in the room.	房有蟲。fóng yáuh chùhng
...doesn't work.	…唔得。...m dāk
Can you fix...?	你可唔可以整…? néih hó m hó yíh jíng…
– the air conditioning	– 冷氣 láahng hei
– the fan	– 風扇 fūng sin
– the heat	– 暖氣 nyúhn hei
– the light	– 燈 dāng
– the TV	– 電視 dihn sih
– the toilet	– 洗手間 sái sáu gāan
I'd like another room.	我想換房。ngóh séung wuhn fóng

Check-out

When's check-out?	幾點退房? géi dím teui fóng
Can I leave my bag here until...?	我可唔可以將個袋留喺呢度…? ngóh hó m hó yíh jēung go dói làuh hái nī douh…

▶ For time, see page 160.

Can I have *an itemized bill/ a receipt*?	你可唔可以畀一張詳細帳單/收據我? néih hó m hó yíh béi yāt jēung chèuhng sai jeung dāan/sāu geui ngóh
I think there's a mistake.	我認為錯咗。 ngóh yihng wàih cho jó
I'll pay *in cash/by credit card*.	我用現金/信用卡畀錢。 ngóh yuhng *yihn gām/seun yuhng kāat* béi chín

Renting

I reserved *an apartment/a room*.	我訂咗一個單位/一間房。 ngóh dehng jó yāt go *dāan wái/yāt gāan fóng*
My name is…	我嘅名係… ngóh ge méng haih…
Can I have the *key/ key card*?	可唔可以畀鎖匙/鎖匙卡我? hó m hó yíh béi *só sìh/só sìh kāat* ngóh
Are there…?	有冇…? yáuh móuh…
– dishes	– 碟 díp
– pillows	– 枕頭 jám tàuh
– sheets	– 床單 chòhng dāan
– towels	– 毛巾 mòuh gān
– utensils	– 餐具 chāan geuih
When do I put out the trash [rubbish]?	我幾時倒垃圾? ngóh géi sìh dóu laahp saap
…is broken.	…壞咗。 …waaih jó
Can you fix…?	你可唔可以整…? néih hó m hó yíh jíng…
– the air conditioner	– 冷氣 láahng hei
– the dishwasher	– 洗碗機 sái wún gēi
– the microwave	– 微波爐 mèih bō lòuh
– the refrigerator	– 冰箱 bīng sēung
– the stove	– 爐 lòuh
– the washing machine	– 洗衣機 sái yī gēi

Household Items

I need…	我需要… ngóh sēui yiu…
– an adapter	– 一個火牛 yāt go fó ngàuh
– aluminum [kitchen] foil	– 錫紙 sehk jí
– a bottle opener	– 瓶瓶器 hōi pìhng hei
– a broom	– 一把帚把 yāt bá sou bá
– a can opener	– 罐頭刀 gun táu dōu
– cleaning supplies	– 清潔用品 chīng git yuhng bán
– a corkscrew	– 開酒器 hōi jáu hei
– detergent	– 清潔劑 chīng git jāi
– dishwashing liquid	– 洗潔精 sái git jīng
– garbage [rubbish] bags	– 垃圾袋 laahp saap dói
– a lightbulb	– 一個燈膽 yāt go dāng dáam
– matches	– 一啲火柴 yāt dī fó chàaih
– a mop	– 一個拖板 yāt go tō báan
– napkins	– 一啲餐巾 yāt dī chāan gān
– paper towels	– 紙巾 jí gān
– plastic wrap [cling film]	– 保鮮紙 bóu sīn jí
– a plunger	– 泵 bām
– scissors	– 一把較剪 yāt bá gaau jín
– a vacuum cleaner	– 一架吸塵機 yāt ga kāp chàhn gēi

▶ For dishes and utensils, see page 67.

▶ For oven temperatures, see page 165.

Hostel

Is there a bed available?	有冇床? yáuh móuh chòhng
Can I have…?	可唔可以畀…我? hó m hó yíh béi…ngóh
– a *single/double* room	– 一間單人/雙人房 yāt gāan *dāan yàhn/ sēung yàhn* fóng
– a blanket	– 一張毯 yāt jēung jīn
– a pillow	– 一個枕頭 yāt go jám tàuh
– sheets	– 床單 chòhng dāan
– a towel	– 一條毛巾 yāt tìuh mòuh gān
Do you have lockers?	有冇衣櫃? yáuh móuh yī gwaih
When do you lock up?	幾點鎖門? géi dím só mùhn
Do I need a membership card?	使唔使會員證? sái m sái wúih yùhn jing
Here's my International Student Card.	呢個係我嘅國際學生證。nī go haih ngóh ge gwok jai hohk sāang jing

Hostels in China provide inexpensive accommodation options. Beds in dorm-style rooms are the least costly choice; private rooms—ranging from singles to rooms for six or more—may also be available but will usually need to be reserved in advance. Be prepared to pay in cash at hostels and other budget accommodations; credit cards are often not accepted, especially at locations in small towns. Hostels in China associated with Hostelling International accept online reservations; these often offer internet service and more. Visit the Hostelling International website for details.

▶ For useful websites, see page 165.

Camping

Can I camp here?	我可唔可以喺呢度露營？ ngóh hó m hó yíh hái nī douh louh yìhng
Where's the campsite?	營地喺邊度？ yìhng deih hái bīn douh
What is the charge per *day/week*?	每日/星期幾多錢？ *múih yaht/sīng kèih* géi dō chín
Are there…?	有冇…? yáuh móuh…
– cooking facilities	– 烹飪設施 pāang yahm chit sī
– electric outlets	– 電掣 dihn jai
– laundry facilities	– 洗衣設施 sái yī chit beih
– showers	– 花灑 fā sá
– tents for rent [hire]	– 出租嘅帳篷 chēut jōu jeung fùhng

You May See...

飲用水 yám yuhng séui	drinking water
禁止野營 gam jí yéh yìhng	no camping
禁止生火/燒烤 gam jí *sāng fó/sīu hāau*	no *fires/barbecues*

▶ For household items, see page 46.

▶ For dishes and utensils, see page 67.

Camping is fairly uncommon in China; most campsites are located near a preserve or other nature attractions. Check with your travel agent or the concierge at your hotel for more information.

Internet and Communications

Essential

Where's an internet cafe?	網吧喺邊度？ móhng bā hái bīn douh
Can I *access the internet/check e-mail*?	我可唔可以上網/查電子郵件？ ngóh hó m hó yíh *séung móhng/chàh dihn jí yáuh gín*
How much per *hour/half hour*?	每個/半個鐘頭幾多錢？ múih *go/bun go* jūng tàuh géi dō chín
How do I connect?	我點樣上網？ ngóh dím yéung séuhng móhng
A phone card, please.	唔該畀一張電話卡我。 m gōi béi yāt jēung dihn wá kāat ngóh
Can I have your phone number?	可唔可以畀你嘅電話號碼我？ hó m hó yíh béi néih ge dihn wá houh máh ngóh
Here's my *number/e-mail*.	呢個係我嘅電話號碼/電郵地址。 nī go haih ngóh ge *dihn wá houh máh/dihn yàuh deih jí*
Call/E-mail me.	打電話/發電郵畀我。 *dá dihn wá/faat dihn yàuh* béi ngóh
Hello. This is…	你好，我係… néih hóu ngóh haih…
Can I speak to…?	我可唔可以同…傾？ ngóh hó m hó yíh tùhng…kīng
Can you repeat that?	你可唔可以重複一次？ néih hó m hó yíh chùhng fūk yāt chi
I'll call back later.	我等一陣再打電話嚟。 ngóh dáng yāt jahn joi dá dihn wá làih
Bye.	再見。 joi gin
Where's the post office?	郵局喺邊度？ yàuh gúk hái bīn douh
I'd like to send these to…	我想將呢啲野送到… ngóh séung jēung nī dī yéh sung dou…

Computer, Internet and E-mail

Where's an internet cafe?	網吧喺邊度?	móhng bā hái bīn douh
Does it have wireless internet?	有冇無線上網?	yáuh móuh mòuh sin séung móhng
How do I turn the computer *on/off*?	點樣開/關電腦?	dím yéung *hōi/gwāan* dihn nouh
Can I…?	我可唔可以…?	ngóh hó m hó yíh…
– access the internet	– 上網	séuhng móhng
– check e-mail	– 查電郵	chàh dihn yàuh
– print	– 列印	liht yan
– use any computer	– 用電腦	yuhng dihn nóuh
How much per (half) hour?	每(半)個鐘頭幾多錢?	múih (bun) go jūng tàuh géi dō chín
How do I…?	點樣…?	dím yéung…
– connect/disconnect	– 連接/斷線	lìhn jip/tyúhn sin
– log on/log off	– 登錄/退出	dāng luhk/teui chēut
– type this symbol	– 輸入呢個符號	syū yahp nī go fùh hóu
What's your e-mail?	你嘅電郵係乜野?	néih ge dihn yàuh haih māt yéh
My e-mail is…	我嘅電郵係…	ngóh ge dihn yàuh haih…

You May See…

關閉 gwāan bai	close
刪除 sāan chèuih	delete
電子郵件 dihn jí yàuh gín	e-mail
退出 teui chēut	exit
幫助 bōng joh	help

聊天 lìuh tīn	instant messenger
互聯網 wuh lyùhn móhng	internet
登錄 dāng luhk	login
新(信息) sān (seun sīk)	new (message)
開/關 hōi/gwāan	on/off
打開 dá hōi	open
列印 liht yan	print
保存 bóu chyùhn	save
送 sung	send
用戶名/密碼 yuhng wuh méng/maht máh	username/password
無線上網 mòuh sin séuhng móhng	wireless internet

i Internet-access centers and cafes can be found in major cities in China. Many hotels offer computer and internet facilities in their business centers as well as wireless internet access in private rooms, usually for a fee.

Phone

A *phone card/prepaid phone*, please.	唔該畀一張電話卡/預付電話卡我。 m gōi béi yāt jēung *dihn wá kāat/yuh fuh dihn wá kāat* ngóh
How much?	幾多錢？géi dō chín
Can I *recharge/buy minutes for* this phone?	我可唔可以幫呢個電話加錢/買多啲分鐘？ngóh hó m hó yíh bōng nī go dihn wá *gā chín/máaih dō dī fān jūng*
My phone doesn't work here.	我嘅電話喺呢度唔用得。ngóh ge dihn wá hái nī douh m yuhng dāk
What's the *area/country* code for…?	…區號/國家代碼係乜野？…*kēui houh/gwok gā doih máh* hahh mãt yéh
What's the number for Information?	訊問台號碼係幾多號？sēun mahn tòih houh máh hahh géi dō houh
I'd like the number for…	我想要…嘅號碼。ngóh séung yiu…ge houh máh
I'd like to call collect [reverse the charges].	我想打對方付費電話。ngóh séung dá deui fōng fuh fún dihn wá
Can I have your number?	可唔可以畀你嘅電話號碼我？hó m hó yíh béi néih ge dihn wá houh máh ngóh
Here's my number.	呢個係我嘅號碼。nī go hahh ngóh ge houh máh

▶ For numbers, see page 157.

Please *call/text* me.	唔該你打電話/發短信畀我。m gōi néih *dá dihn wá/faat dyún seun* béi ngóh
I'll *call/text* you.	我會打電話/發短信畀你。ngóh wúih *dá dihn wá/faat dyún seun* béi néih

52

On the Phone

Hello. This is…	你好。我係… néih hóu ngóh haih…
Can I speak to…?	我可唔可以同…傾? ngóh hó m hó yíh tùhng…kīng
Extension…	唔該你轉… m gōi néih jyun…
Speak *louder/more slowly*, please.	唔該你大聲/慢慢講。 m gōi néih *daaih sēng/maahn máan* góng
Can you repeat that?	你可唔可以再講? néih hó m hó yíh joi góng
I'll call back later.	我之後再打 ngóh jī hauh joi dá
Bye.	再見。 joi gin

You May Hear…

你係邊位? néih haih bīn wái	Who's calling?
唔該等一等。 m gōi dáng yāt dáng	Hold on.
我幫你接。 ngóh bōng néih jip	I'll put you through.
佢唔喺度/接緊另一個電話。 kéuih *m hái douh/jip gán lihng yāt go dihn wá*	He/She is *not here/ on another line.*
你使不使留言? néih sái m sái làuh yìhn	Would you like to leave a message?
之後/十分鐘後再打。 jī hauh/sahp fān jūng hauh joi dá	Call back *later/in 10 minutes.*
佢可唔可以打電話畀你? kéuih hó m hó yíh dá dihn wá béi néih	Can he/she call you back?
你幾號電話? néih géi houh dihn wá	What's your number?

Public phones can be found in most cities in China but rarely in remote areas. These phones are usually coin-operated; some may be designed for use with credit cards or phone cards, which can be purchased from grocery stores, convenience stores or newsstands. For a better rate, make your international call from calling centers or stalls, available in larger cities. Local calls inside China, including at hotels, are often free of charge. Calls from Hong Kong to other cities in China and Macau are considered long-distance calls. Avoid making international calls from hotels, where high surcharges are added to the already high cost of the call.

For national calls, dial 0 + area code + the phone number.
For calls to the U.S. or Canada, dial 00 + 1 + area code + phone number.
For calls to the U.K., dial 00 + 44 + area code + phone number.

Fax

Can I *send/receive* a fax here?	呢度可唔可以發/接傳真？ nī douh hó m hó yíh *faat/sāu* chyùhn jān

| What's the fax number? | 傳真號係幾多？ chyùhn jān houh máh haih géi dō |
| Please fax this to… | 唔該你將呢個傳真畀… m gōi néih jēung nī go chyùhn jān béi… |

Post Office

Where's the *post office/mailbox [postbox]*?	郵局/郵箱喺邊度？ yàuh gúk/yàuh sēung hái bīn douh
A stamp for this *postcard/letter* to…	一張將呢張明信片/封信寄到…嘅郵票。 yāt jēung jēung nī jēung *mìhng seun pín/fūng seun* gei dou…ge yàuh piu
How much?	幾多？ géi dō
Send this package *by airmail/express.*	用航空/用快件寄呢個包裹 yuhng *hòhng hūng/yuhng faai gín* gei nī go bāau gwó
A receipt, please.	唔該你畀收據我。 m gōi néih béi sāu geui ngóh

You May Hear…

填好海關申報表。 tìhn hóu hói gwāan sān bou bíu	Fill out the customs declaration form.
價值係幾多？ ga jihk haih géi dō	What's the value?
裏面裝啲乜野？ léuih mihn jōng dī māt yéh	What's inside?

Post offices can be found throughout China. They normally provide express, registered, overnight and general mail service. Additionally, they may also take payment on behalf of utility companies. Online postal services are available; you can mail your packages, track their status, wire money, order merchandise and pay your utility bills.

▼ Food

Essential

Can you recommend a good *restaurant/bar*?	你可唔可以介紹一間好嘅餐廳/酒吧? néih hó m hó yíh gaai siuh yāt gāan hóu ge *chāan tēng/jáu bā*
Is there *a traditional Chinese/an inexpensive* restaurant nearby?	附近有冇傳統嘅中國/唔貴嘅餐廳? fuh gahn yáuh móuh *chyùhn túng ge jūng gwok/m gwai* ge chāan tēng
A table for *one/two*, please.	唔該畀一/兩人嘅檯我。 m gōi béi *yāt/léuhng* yàhn ge tói ngóh
Can we sit…?	我哋可唔可以坐喺…? ngóh deih hó m hó yíh chóh hái…
– here/there	– 呢度/嗰度 nī douh/gó douh
– outside	– 外面 ngoih mihn
– in a non-smoking area	– 禁煙區 gam yīn kēui
I'm waiting for someone.	我等緊人。 ngóh dáng gán yàhn
Where's the restroom [toilet]?	洗手間喺邊度? sái sáu gāan hái bīn douh
A menu, please.	唔該你畀菜牌我。 m gōi néih béi choi páai ngóh
What do you recommend?	你介紹乜野菜呢? néih gaai siuh māt yéh choi nē
I'd like…	我想要… ngóh séung yiu…
Some more…, please.	唔該你再畀一啲…我。 m gōi néih joi béi yāt dī…ngóh
Enjoy your meal!	慢用! maahn yuhng

The check [bill], please.	唔該埋單。 m gōi màaih dāan
Is service included?	包唔包服務費? bāau m bāau fuhk mouh fai
Can I pay by credit card?	我可唔可以用信用卡畀錢? ngóh hó m hó yíh yuhng seun yuhng kāat béi chín
Can I have a receipt?	我可唔可以要一張收據? ngóh hó m hó yíh yiu yāt jēung sāu geui
Thank you!	多謝! dō jeh

Restaurant Types

Can you recommend...?	你可唔可以介紹…? néih hó m hó yíh gaai siuh…
– a restaurant	– 一間餐廳 yāt gāan chāan tēng
– a bar	– 一間酒吧 yāt gāan jáu bā
– a cafe	– 一間咖啡室 yāt gāan ga fē sāt
– a fast-food place	– 一間快餐店 yāt gāan faai chāan dim
– a snack bar	– 一間小食店 yāt gāan síu sihk dim
– a teahouse	– 一間茶樓 yāt gāan chàh làuh

Authentic Chinese food should be one of the highlights of your trip. By Chinese tradition, food should be filling and have a healing effect; a Chinese meal is based on balance. In addition to Chinese eateries, Korean and Japanese restaurants are popular as are international fast-food restaurants.

Because of size of the country, Chinese cuisine varies greatly from region to region. The main styles are:

Beijing (Northern) cuisine
Wheat, not rice, is the staple in northern China, so Beijing cuisine is comprised mainly of noodles, steamed bread and

dumplings. Beijing is the place to order Peking duck, a roasted, crisy-skinned duck wrapped in wafer-thin pancake with spring onions and sweet bean sauce.

Cantonese (Southern) cuisine

The majority of Chinese restaurants outside of China feature Cantonese-style cooking, so you will likely be familiar with the dishes and flavors. Steaming and stir-frying are the signatures of Cantonese cooking; these methods preserve the food's natural colors, flavors and vitamins. Rice, steamed or stir-fried, is the traditional accompaniment to a Cantonese-style meal.

Hunan (Central) cuisine

Chili pepper is a popular spice here, as in the neighboring Sichuan region, home of Szechuan cuisine. Hunan cuisine is known for rich sweet-and-sour sauces. Smoked and cured food is also popular.

Shanghai (Eastern) cuisine

Seafood and vegetable dishes abound, since this cuisine is based around the coastal areas of Shanghai. Be sure to sample the steamed freshwater crab, honey-fried eel, yellowfish and sautéed shrimp.

Szechuan (Western) cuisine

This province is well-known for its hot, peppery dishes. Food is not just spicy; Szechuan cooking combines a number of flavors: bitter, sweet, tart and sour.

The Chinese tend to eat early. Breakfast, 早餐 **jóu chāan**, is usually served from 6–8 a.m. and lunch, 晏晝 **ngaan jau**, from 11 a.m.–1 p.m. You probably won't be able to order dinner, 晚飯 **máahn faahn**, past 8 p.m., except in the south, where social life continues until late in the evening. Chinese meals are enjoyed in a group. Tables often have revolving platforms so the various dishes can be shared; using chopsticks lengthens the reach.

Reservations and Questions

I'd like to reserve a table…	我想訂一張…嘅檯。 ngóh séung dehng yāt jēung…ge tói
– for two	– 兩個人 léuhng go yàhn
– for this evening	– 今晚 gām māan
– for tomorrow at…	– 聽日… tīng yaht…
A table for two, please.	唔該畀一張兩個人嘅檯我 m gōi béi yāt jēung léuhng go yàhn ge tói ngóh
We have a reservation.	我哋有訂檯。 ngóh deih yáuh dehng tói
My name is…	我嘅名係… ngóh ge méng haih…
Can we sit…?	我哋可唔可以坐喺…? ngóh deih hó m hó yíh chóh hái…
– here/there	– 呢度/嗰度 nī douh/gó douh
– outside	– 外面 ngoh mihn
– in a non-smoking area	– 禁煙區 gam yīn kēui
– by the window	– 近窗口 gahn chēung háu
Where's the restroom [toilet]?	洗手間喺邊度? sái sáu gāan hái bīn douh

You May Hear...

你有冇訂枱? néih yáuh móuh dehng tói		Do you have a reservation?
幾多人? géi dō yàhn		How many?
吸煙區定係禁煙區? kāp yīn kēui dihng gam yīn kēui		Smoking or non-smoking?
你可以叫野未? néih hó yíh giu yéh meih		Are you ready to order?
你想食乜野呢? néih séung sihk māt yéh nē		What would you like?
我介紹… ngóhgaai siuh…		I recommend…
慢慢食。 maahn máan sihk		Enjoy your meal.

Ordering

Waiter/Waitress!	伙記! fó gei
We're ready to order.	我哋可以叫野喇。 ngóh deih hó yíh giu yéh la
The wine list, please.	唔該畀酒牌我。 m gōi béi jáu páai ngóh
I'd like…	我想要… ngóh séung yiu…
– a bottle of…	– 一樽… yāt jēun…
– a carafe of…	– 一碴… yāt jā…
– a glass of…	– 一杯… yāt būi…

▶ For alcoholic and non-alcoholic drinks, see page 78.

The menu, please.	唔該你畀菜牌我。 m gōi néih béi choi páai ngóh
Do you have a *menu in English/children's menu*?	你係唔係有英文菜牌/兒童菜牌? néih haih m haih yáuh *yīng màhn choi páai/yìh tùhng choi páai*
What do you recommend?	你介紹乜野? néih gaai siuh māt yéh
What's this?	呢啲係乜野? nī dī haih māt yéh

What's in it?	裏面有乜野? léuih mihn yáuh māt yéh
Is it spicy?	辣唔辣? laaht m laaht
Without..., please.	唔該唔好落… m gōi m hóu lohk…
It's to go [take away].	我要拎走。 ngóh yiu nīng jáu

You May See...

附加費 fuh gā fai	cover charge
固定價格 gu dihng ga gaak	fixed-price
菜單 choi dāan	menu
當日菜單 dōng yaht choi dāan	menu of the day
(不) 包括服務費 (bāt) bāau kwut fuhk mouh fai	service (not) included
配菜 pui choi	side dishes
特色菜 dahk sīk choi	specials

Cooking Methods

baked	烤 hāau
boiled	煮 jyú
braised	燜 mān
creamed	提取乳脂 tàih chéui yúh jī
diced	切成細塊 chit sìhng sai faai
fileted	去骨切片 heui gwāt chit pín
fried	煎 jīn
grilled	烤 hāau
poached	水煮 séui jyú
roasted	烤 hāau
sautéed	炒 cháau
smoked	薰 fān
steamed	蒸 jīng

stewed	燉 dahn
stuffed	有餡 yáuh háam

Special Requirements

I'm…	我係… ngóh haih…
– diabetic	– 糖尿病患者 tòhng liuh behng waahn jé
– lactose intolerant	– 乳糖過敏者 yúh tòhng gwo mán jé
– vegetarian	– 素食者 sou sihk jé
I'm allergic to…	我對…敏感。 ngóh deui…máhn gám
I can't eat…	我唔食得… ngóh m̀ sihk dāk…
– dairy	– 乳製品 yúh jai bán
– gluten	– 麵筋 mihn gān
– nuts	– 硬殼果 ngaahng hok gwó
– pork	– 豬肉 jyū yuhk
– shellfish	– 貝類 bui leuih
– spicy foods	– 辣 laaht
– wheat	– 麵 mihn
Is it *halal/kosher*?	呢啲係唔係清真食品/猶太食品？ nī dī haih m̀ haih *chīng jān sihk bán/yàuh taai sihk bán*

Dining with Kids

Do you have children's portions?	你哋有冇兒童餐？ néih deih yáuh móuh yìh tùhng chāan
A *highchair/child's seat*, please.	唔該畀一張高凳/BB凳我。 m̀ gōi béi yāt jēung *gōu dang/bìh bī dang* ngóh
Where can I *feed/change* the baby?	我喺邊度可以餵BB/幫BB換尿片？ ngóh hái bīn douh hó yíh *wai bìh bī/bōng bìh bī wuhn liuh pín*
Can you warm this?	你可唔可以加熱？ néih hó m̀ hó yíh gā yiht

▶ For travel with children, see page 136.

Complaints

How much longer will our food be?	仲要幾耐時間幫我哋上菜？juhng yiu géi noih sìh gaan bōng ngóh deih séung choi
We can't wait any longer.	我哋唔可以再等喇。ngóh deih m hó yíh joi dáng la
We're leaving.	我哋要走喇。ngóh deih yiu jáu la
I didn't order this.	我冇叫呢碟菜。ngóh móuh giu nī dihp choi
I ordered…	我叫咗… ngóh giu jó…
I can't eat this.	呢個唔食得。nī go m sihk dāk
This is too…	呢個太… nī go taai…
– cold/hot	– 凍/熱 dung/yiht
– salty/spicy	– 鹹/辣 hàahm/laaht
– tough/bland	– 硬/淡 ngaahng/táahm
This isn't *clean/fresh*.	呢個唔乾淨/新鮮。nī go m *gōn jehng/sān sīn*

Paying

The check [bill], please.	埋單。màaih dāan
Separate checks [bills], please.	分開畀。fān hōi béi
It's all together.	一齊畀。yāt chàih béi
Is service included?	包唔包服務費？bāau m bāau fuhk mouh fai
What's this amount for?	呢啲係乜野費用？nī dī haih māt yéh fai yuhng
I didn't have that. I had…	我冇食呢個。我食嘅係… ngóh móuh sihk nī go ngóh sihk ge haih…

Can I have *an itemized bill/ a receipt*?	你可唔可以畀一張詳細帳單/收據我？ néih hó m hó yíh béi yāt jēung chèuhng sai *jeung dāan/sāu geui* ngóh
That was delicious!	呢個好好食！ nī go hóu hóu sihk

i Tipping is not expected nor is it compulsory in China, though, in Hong Kong, it is fairly common. Service charges may apply in some restaurants, especially those that offer private rooms. You won't see tax included on the bill; there is no sales tax in China.

Market

Where are the *carts [trolleys]/baskets*?	手推車/購物籃喺邊度？ sáu tēui chē/kau maht láam hái bī douh
Where is...?	…喺邊度？ ...hái bīn douh

▶ For food items, see page 82.

I'd like some of *that/ this*.	我想要嗰個/呢個。 ngóh séung yiudī *gó go/nī go*
Can I taste it?	我可唔可以試吓？ ngóh hó m hó yíh si háh
I'd like...	我想要… ngóh séung yiu...
– a *kilo/half-kilo* of...	– 一公斤/半公斤… yāt gūng gān/bun gūng gān...
– a liter of...	– 一升… yāt sīng...
– a *piece/slice* of...	– 一塊… yāt faai...
More/Less.	多啲/少啲。 dō dī/síu dī
How much?	幾多錢？ géi dō chín
Where do I pay?	我喺邊度畀錢？ ngóh hái bīn douh béi chín
A bag, please.	唔該畀一個袋我。 m gōi béi yāt go dói ngóh
I'm being helped.	有人幫我喇。 yáuh yàhn bōng ngóh la

▶ For conversion tables, see page 163.

You May Hear...

我可唔可以幫你？ ngóh hó m hó yíh bōng néih	Can I help you?
你想要乜野？ néih séung yiu māt yéh	What would you like?
仲要唔要第二啲？ juhng yiu m yiu daih yih dī	Anything else?
嗰啲係港幣。 gó dī haih góng baih	That's…Hong Kong dollars.

i In major cities in China, you'll find supermarkets selling a variety of goods, often imported, as well as food items. Most food shopping is done at local markets, where fresh meat, fish, fruit and vegetables can be found. Small grocery stores and convenience stores sell various goods, including cooking spices, sauces, etc. You may also be able to purchase cigars and liquor at these stores.

You May See...

過期日 gwo kèih yaht	expiration date
卡路里 kā louh léih	calories
無脂肪 mòuh jī fōng	fat free
需冷藏 sēui láahng chòhng	keep refrigerated
含有微量… hàhm yáuh mèih leuhng…	may contain traces of…
微波爐可用 mèih bō lòuh hó yuhng	microwaveable
喺…之前出售 hái…jī chìhn chēut sauh	sell by…
適合素食者 sīk hahp sou sihk jé	suitable for vegetarians

Dishes, Utensils and Kitchen Tools

bottle opener	開瓶器 hōi pìhng hei
bowl	碗 wún
can opener	罐頭刀 gun táu dōu
ceramic spoon	湯羹 tōng gāng
clay pot	沙鍋 sā wō
corkscrew	開酒器 hōi jáu hei
cup	杯 būi
fork	叉 chā
frying pan	鑊 wohk
glass	玻璃杯 bō lēi būi
knife	餐刀 chāan dōu
napkin	餐巾 chāan gān
plate	碟 díp
pot	鍋 wō
spatula	鏟 cháan
spoon	瓷羹 chìh gāng
steamer	蒸鍋 jīng wō
wok	鑊 wohk

Meals

Breakfast

bacon	鹹肉 hàahm yuhk
bread	麵包 mihn bāau
butter	牛油 ngàuh yàuh
cereal	麥片 mahk pín
cheese	芝士 jī sí
coffee/tea…	…咖啡/茶 …ga fē/chàh
– black	– 黑 hāk
– decaf	– 無咖啡因嘅 mòuh ga fē yān ge
– with milk	– 加牛奶 gā ngàuh náaih
– with sugar	– 加糖 gā tòhng
– with artificial sweetener	– 加代糖 gā doih tòhng
deep-fried dough sticks	油炸鬼 yàuh ja gwái
egg, fried	煎蛋 jīn dáan
egg, *hard-/soft*-boiled	蛋煮得老/嫩 dáan jyú dāk *lóuh/nyuhn*
egg, hard-boiled in tea-leaf water	茶葉蛋 chàh yihp dáan
jam	果占 gwó jīm
jelly	喏厘 jē léi
…juice	…汁 …jāp
– apple	– 蘋果 pìhng gwó
– grapefruit	– 西柚 sāi yáu

I'd like…	我想要… ngóh séung yiu…
More…, please.	唔該我想再要… m gōi ngóh séung joi yiu…

– orange	– 橙 cháang
milk	牛奶 ngàauh náaih
oatmeal	麥皮 mahk pèih
omelet	菴列 ngām liht
rice porridge	粥 jūk
sausage	香腸 hēung chéung
sesame seed cake	芝麻燒餅 jī màh sīu béng
soy milk	豆奶 dauh náaih
steamed bun	饅頭 maahn tàuh
steamed, stuffed bun	包 bāau
toast	多士 dō sí
yogurt	乳酪 yúh lohk
water	水 séui

Continental breakfast is served at most hotels that cater to Europeans and Americans. If you prefer a Chinese breakfast, your meal will usually be comprised of rice or wheat porridge, to which almost anything can be added: fried dough, salted fish, etc. Noodle soup with pieces of pork and/or vegetables is another popular Chinese breakfast.

Appetizers [Starters]

chicken feet	鳳爪 fuhng jáau
cold jellyfish in sauce	涼拌海蜇皮 lèuhng buhn hói jit pèih
cold stewed beef in sauce	鹵牛肉 lóuh ngàuh yuhk
crispy vinegar cucumber	涼拌黃瓜 lèuhng buhn wòhng gwā

With/Without…	加/唔加… gā/m gā…
I can't have…	我唔食得… ngóh m sihk dāk…

pickles	泡菜 paau choi
preserved egg	皮蛋 pèih dáan
shrimp with salt and pepper	椒鹽蝦 jīu yìhm hā
sliced ham	火腿 fó téui
smoked meat	薰肉 fān yuhk
spring roll	春卷 chēun gyún
steamed bun	蒸包 jīng bāau
steamed dumplings	蒸餃 jīng gáau

| I'd like… | 我想要… ngóh séung yiu… |
| More…, please. | 唔該我想再要… m gōi ngóh séung joi yiu… |

Chinese appetizers are ordered before a meal. In many restaurants, you can order a platter of a different appetizers, which are mostly cold dishes.

Soup

...soup	…湯 …tōng
– bean curd	– 豆腐 dauh fuh
– chicken	– 雞 gāi
– corn and egg	– 粟米蛋 sūk máih dáan
– egg drop	– 蛋花 daahn fā
– hot and sour	– 酸辣 syūn laaht
– meat, seafood and egg	– 三鮮 sāam sīn
– pork	– 肉絲 yuhk sī
– seafood	– 海鮮 hói sīn
– spare rib	– 排骨 pàaih gwāt
– squid	– 魷魚 yàuh yú
– tomato	– 蕃茄 fāan ké
– vegetable	– 菜 choi

 When in China, you may wish to follow Chinese etiquette. Sip your soup directly from the soup bowl or use the ceramic soup spoon provided. Elbows remain on the table and bowls are lifted off the table while enjoying the soup.

With/Without...	加/唔加…	gā/m gā...
I can't have...	我唔食得…	ngóh m sihk dāk...

Egg Dishes

eggs with Chinese chives	韭菜炒雞蛋 gáu choi cháau gāi dáan
eggs with cucumber	黃瓜炒雞蛋 wòhng gwā cháau gāi dáan
eggs with a mixture of chopped meat and vegetables	芙蓉蛋 fùh yùhng dáan
eggs with peeled freshwater shrimp	蝦仁炒蛋 hā yàhn cháau dáan
pickled egg	皮蛋 pèih dáan
steamed egg	蒸蛋 jīng dáan

Tofu Dishes

breaded tofu	鍋塌豆腐 wō taap dauh fuh
cold tofu with garlic sauce	涼拌豆腐 lèuhng buhn dauh fuh
crushed tofu with pickled egg	皮蛋豆腐 pèih dáan dauh fuh
fried, stuffed tofu	鍋貼豆腐 wō tip dauh fuh
spicy tofu	麻婆豆腐 màh pòh dauh fuh
tofu in a clay pot	沙鍋豆腐 sā wō dauh fuh
tofu with fish	魚片豆腐 yùh pín dauh fuh
tofu with meatballs	肉丸豆腐 yuhk yún dauh fuh
tofu with peeled freshwater shimp	蝦仁豆腐 hā yàhn dauh fuh

I'd like…	我想要… ngóh séung yiu…
More…, please.	唔該我想再要… m gōi ngóh séung joi yiu…

Fish and Seafood

clam	蜆 hín
cod	鱈魚 syut yú
crab	蟹 háaih
crucian carp	鯽魚 jāk yú
grass carp	草魚 chóu yú
hairtail	帶魚 daai yú
halibut	大比目魚 daaih béi muhk yú
herring	鯡魚 pàaih yú
lobster	龍蝦 lùhng hā
octopus	章魚 jēung yùh
oyster	蠔 hòuh
salmon	三文魚 sāam màhn yú
sea bass	鱸魚 lòuh yú
shrimp	蝦 hā
silver carp	鰱魚 lìhn yú
sole	板魚 báan yú
squid	魷魚 yàuh yú
swordfish	劍魚 gim yú
trout	鱒魚 jēun yú
tuna	金槍魚 gām chōng yú

With/Without…	加/唔加… gā/m gā…
I can't have…	我唔食得… ngóh m sihk dāk…

Meat and Poultry

beef	牛肉 ngàuh yuhk
chicken	雞肉 gāi yuhk
cured pork	鹹肉 hàahm yuhk
duck	鴨肉 ngaap yuhk
ham	火腿 fó téui
heart (pork)	(豬) 心 (jyū) sām
kidney (pork)	(豬) 腰 (jyū) yīu
lamb	羊肉 yèuhng yuhk
liver	豬肝 jyū gōn
oxen entrails	牛雜 ngàuh jaahp
oxen tripe	牛柏葉 ngàuh paak yihp
pork	豬肉 jyū yuhk
pork tripe	豬肚 jyū tóuh
rabbit	兔肉 tou yuhk
sausage	香腸 hēung chéung
spare ribs	豬扒 jyū pá
steak	牛扒 ngàuh pá

Vegetables and Staples

asparagus	露筍 louh séun
broccoli	西蘭花 sāi làahn fā
cabbage	椰菜 yèh choi
carrot	紅蘿蔔 hùhng lòh baahk
cauliflower	菜心 choi sām
celery	芹菜 kàhn choi
Chinese cabbage	白菜 baahk choi

I'd like…	我想要… ngóh séung yiu…
More…, please.	唔該我想再要… m gōi ngóh séung joi yiu…

Chinese long bean	荷蘭豆 hòh lāan dáu
Chinese water spinach	通菜 tūng choi
corn	粟米 sūk máih
eggplant [aubergine]	矮瓜 ngái gwā
garlic	蒜 syun
green bean	扁豆 bín dáu
leaf mustard	芥菜 gaai choi
lettuce	生菜 sāang choi
mushroom	蘑菇 mòh gū
noodles	麵 mihn
nori (type of seaweed)	紫菜 jí choi
olive	橄欖 gaam láam
pea	豆 dáu
potato	薯仔 syùh jái
radish	蘿蔔 lòh baahk
red/green pepper	紅/青椒 hùhng/chēng jīu
rice	米 máih
scallion	大蔥 daaih syun
seaweed	海帶 hói daai
soy bean	黃豆 wòhng dáu
spinach	菠菜 bō choi
tofu	豆腐 dauh fuh
tomato	蕃茄 fāan ké
vegetable	菜 choi

With/Without…	加/唔加… gā/m gā…
I can't have…	我唔食得… ngóh m sihk dāk…

i The proper way to eat a bowl of rice is to hold the bowl up with one hand and push the rice into your mouth with chopsticks. Do not stick the chopsticks upright into a bowl of rice; this is considered an ominous sign as it resembles incense sticks burned for funerals or at shrines. When finished with your meal, rest the chopsticks across the top of the bowl; some people will place the chopsticks on the table when they finish the meal.

Fruit

apple	蘋果	pìhng gwó
apricot	杏	hahng
banana	香蕉	hēung jīu
cherry	車厘子	chē lèih jí
Chinese dates	棗	jóu
crab apple	山碴	sāan jā
fruit	生果	sāang gwó
grape	提子	tàih jí
grapefruit	西柚	sāi yáu
kiwi	奇異果	kèih yih gwó
lemon	檸檬	nìhng mūng
lime	青檸	chēng níng
longan fruit	龍眼	lùhng ngáahn
lychee	荔枝	laih jī
mandarin orange	柑	gām

I'd like…	我想要… ngóh séung yiu…
More…, please.	唔該我想再要… m gōi ngóh séung joi yiu…

mango	芒果 mōng gwó
melon	蜜瓜 maht gwā
orange	橙 cháang
peach	桃 tóu
pear	梨 léih
pineapple	菠籮 bō lòh
plum	李 léih
pomegranate	石榴 sehk láu
red bayberry	楊梅 yèuhng múi
strawberry	草莓/士多啤厘 chóu múi/sih dō bē léi

Dessert

| mixed fruit | 生果 sāang gwó |
| sweetened red bean paste | 紅豆沙 hùhng dáu sā |

The Chinese rarely finish a meal with dessert but, instead, have fruit. In general sweets are eaten as snacks. You can buy desserts at bakeries and teahouses; some supermarkets have a section for desserts as well.

| With/Without... | 加/唔加… gā/m gā… |
| I can't have... | 我唔食得… ngóh m sihk dāk… |

Drinks

Essential

The wine list please.	唔該畀酒牌我。 m gōi béi jáu páai ngóh
What do you recommend?	你介紹乜野？ néih gaai siuh māt yéh
I'd like a *bottle/glass* of *red/white* wine.	我想要一樽/杯紅/白酒。 ngóh séung yiu yāt jēun/būi hùhng/baahk jáu
Another *bottle/glass*, please.	唔該再畀一樽/杯我。 m gōi joi béi yāt jēun/būi ngóh
I'd like a local beer.	我想飲當地嘅啤酒。 ngóh séung yám dōng deih ge bē jáu
Can I buy you a drink?	我可唔可以請你飲？ ngóh hó m hó yíh chéng néih yám
Cheers!	乾杯！ gōn būi
A *coffee/tea*, please.	唔該畀一杯咖啡/茶我。 m gōi béi yāt būi ga fē/chàh ngóh
Black.	黑 hāk
With…	加… gā…
– milk	– 牛奶 ngàuh náaih
– sugar	– 糖 tòhng
– artificial sweetener	– 代糖 doih tòhng
…, please.	唔該畀一杯…我。 m gōi béi yāt būi…ngóh
– Juice	– 果汁 gwó jāp
– Soda	– 蘇打水 sō dá séui
– *Sparkling/Still* water	– 有汽/蒸餾水 yáuh hei/jīng lauh séui
Is the water safe to drink?	呢啲水可唔可以飲？ nī dī séui hó m hó yíh yám

Non-alcoholic Drinks

coffee	咖啡 ga fē
cola	可樂 hó lohk
hot chocolate	熱朱古力 yiht jyū gū līk
juice	果汁 gwó jāp
…tea	…茶 …chàh
– green	– 綠 luhk
– jasmine	– 茉莉花 muht léih fā
– lemon	– 檸檬 nìhng mūng
– milk	– 奶 náaih
– oolong	– 烏龍 wū lúng
milk	牛奶 ngàuh náaih
soda	蘇打水 sō dá séui
soymilk	豆奶 dauh náaih
sparkling/still water	有汽/蒸餾水 *yáuh hei/jīng lauh* séui

i Tea is the most popular beverage in China. Though teahouses are not as common as they once were, they are still an ideal location to sample the traditional drink, enjoyed without milk or sugar. In most hotel rooms are flasks with hot water and green or black teabags.

Ground coffee is hard to find, though instant coffee is generally available.

Do not drink water directly from the tap. Instead, try mineral water or Chinese soft drinks—generally very sweet—which are sold everywhere. Milk can be found in supermarkets, but soy milk is more popular and might be a suitable alternative for you.

You May Hear...

我可唔可以請你飲野？	ngóh hó m hó yíh chéng néíh yám yéh	Can I get you a drink?
加牛奶定係加糖？	gā ngàuh náaih dihng haih gā tòhng	With milk or sugar?
有汽水定係蒸餾水？	yáuh hei séui dihng haih jīng lauh séui	Sparkling or still water?

Aperitifs, Cocktails and Liqueurs

brandy	白蘭地酒	baahk lāan déi jáu
Chinese liqueurs	白酒	baahk jáu
gin	氈酒	jīn jáu
rum	林酒	lām jáu
scotch	蘇格蘭威士忌酒	sōu gaak làahn wāi sih géi
tequila	龍舌蘭酒	lùhng sit làahn jáu

| vodka | 伏特加酒 fuhk dahk gā jáu |
| whisky | 威士忌酒 wāi sih géi jáu |

Beer

beer	啤酒 bē jáu
bottled/draft	樽/生 jēung/sāang
dark/light	黑/淡 hāk/táahm
local/imported	當地/進口 dōng deih/jeun háu
Tsingtao® beer	青島啤酒 chīng dóu bē jáu

Wine

wine	葡萄酒 pòuh tòuh jáu
champagne	香檳 hēung bān
red/white	紅酒/白酒 hùhng jáu/baahk jáu
table	餐酒 chāan jáu
sparkling	汽酒 hei jáu
dessert wine	飯後甜酒 faahn hauh tìhm jáu

---

i Though the Chinese are not widely known for their alcoholic drinks, there is a surprisingly large choice on offer. Wine has been made in China for thousands of years; each region has its own speciality, usually made from rice, fruit, flowers or herbs. Chinese wine is generally sweet.

Tsingtao® is a popular Chinese beer, brewed from the spring water of the Laoshan mountain. You may wish to try a local beer, too; each region has its own.

Chinese liqueurs are often infused with local favorites such as bamboo leaves, chrysanthemum and cloves. Most famous spirits include: 茅台酒 **màauh tòih jáu** and 五粮液 **ngh lèuhng yihk**.

almond	杏仁 hahng yàhn
anchovy	鯷魚 sìh yúh
aperitif	開胃酒 hōi waih jáu
apple	蘋果 pìhng gwó
apricot	杏 hahng
artificial sweetener	代糖 doih tòhng
asparagus	露筍 louh séun
avocado	牛油果 ngàuh yàuh gwó
banana	香蕉 hēung jīu
bass	鱸魚 lòuh yú
bay leaf	月桂葉 yuht gwai yihp
bean	豆 dáu
bean sprout	芽菜 ngàh choi
beef	牛肉 ngàuh yuhk
beer	啤酒 bē jáu
brandy	白蘭地酒 baahk lāan déi jáu
bread	麵包 mihn bāau
breast (of chicken)	雞胸肉 gāi hūng yuhk
broth	湯 tōng
butter	牛油 ngàuh yàuh
buttermilk	乳酪 yúh lohk
cabbage	椰菜 yèh choi
cake	蛋糕 daahn gōu
candy [sweets]	糖 tóng
caramel	焦糖 jīu tòhng

caraway	茴茜 yìhm sāi
carrot	蘿蔔 lòh baahk
cashew	腰果 yīu gwó
cauliflower	菜心 choi sām
celery	芹菜 kàhn choi
cereal	穀物 gūk maht
cheese	芝士 jī sí
cherry	士多啤厘 sih dō bē léi
chervil	細葉芹 sai yihp kàhn
chestnut	栗子 leuht jí
chicken	雞肉 gāi yuhk
chili pepper	辣椒 laaht jīu

Chinese dates	棗 jóu
Chinese liquor	白酒 baahk jáu
chives	香蔥 hēung chūng
chocolate	朱古力 jyū gū līk
chop	斬 jáam
chopped meat	肉餡 yuhk háam
cider	蘋果汁 pìhng gwó jāp
cilantro [coriander]	香菜 hēung choi
cinnamon	肉桂 yuhk gwai
clam	蜆 hín
clove	丁香 dīng hēung
coconut	椰子 yèh jí
cod	鱈魚 syut yú
coffee	咖啡 ga fē
consommé	清燉肉湯 chīng dahn yuhk tōng
cookie [biscuit]	曲奇 kūk kèih
crab	蟹 háaih
crab apple	山碴 sāan jā
crabmeat	蟹肉 háaih yuhk
cracker	餅乾 béng gōn
cream	奶油 náaih yàuh
cream, whipped	發泡奶油 faat póu náaih yàuh
cream cheese	芝士 jī sí
crucian carp	鯽魚 jāak yú
cucumber	青瓜 chēng gwā
cumin	茴茜 yìhm sāi
cured pork	鹹肉 hàahm yuhk
custard	蒸蛋 jīng dáan

dessert wine	飯後甜酒 faahn hauh tìhm jáu
duck	鴨肉 ngaap yuhk
dumpling	餃子 gáau jí
eel	鰻魚 maahn yú
egg	雞蛋 gāi dáan
egg *yolk/white*	蛋黃/蛋白 dáan wóng/dáan baahk
eggplant [aubergine]	矮瓜 ngái gwā
fig	無花果 mòuh fā gwó
fish	魚 yú
French fries	炸薯條 ja syùh tíu
fritter	油炸餡餅 yàuh ja háam béng
fruit	生果 sāang gwó
game	野味 yéh méi
garlic	蒜 syun
garlic sauce	蒜香汁 syun hēung jāp
gin	氈酒 jīn jáu
ginger	薑 gēung
goat	羊肉 yèuhng yuhk
goose	鵝肉 ngòh yuhk
gooseberry	鵝莓 ngòh múi
grapefruit	西柚 sāi yáu
grapes	提子 tàih jí
grass carp	草魚 chóu yú
green bean	青豆 chēng dáu
guava	石榴 sehk láu
haddock	黑線鱈 hāk sin syut
hake	無鬚鱈 mòuh sōu syut
halibut	大比目魚 daaih béi muhk yú

ham	火腿 fó téui
hamburger	漢堡包 hon bóu bāau
hazelnut	榛子 jēun jí
heart	心臟 sām johng
hen	母雞 móuh gāi
herring	鯡魚 pàaih yú
honey	蜂蜜 fūng maht
hot dog	熱狗 yiht gáu
hot pepper sauce	辣醬 laaht jeung
ice (cube)	冰 bīng
ice cream	雪糕 syut gōu
jam	果占 gwó jīm
jelly	啫喱 jē léi
juice	果汁 gwó jāp
ketchup	茄汁 ké jāp
kid (young goat)	小羊肉 síu yèuhng yuhk
kidney	腰 yīu
kiwi	奇異果 kèih yih gwó
lamb	羊肉 yèuhng yuhk
leg	大腿肉 daaih téui yuhk
lemon	檸檬 nìhng mūng
lemonade	檸檬水 nìhng mūng séui
lentil	扁豆 bín dáu
lettuce	生菜 sāang choi
lime	青檸 chēng níng
liver	肝 gōn
lobster	龍蝦 lùhng hā
longan fruit	龍眼 lùhng ngáahn

macaroni	通心粉 tūng sām fán
mackerel	鯖魚 chīng yú
mandarin orange	柑 gām
mango	芒果 mōng gwó
margarine	沙律醬 sā léut jeung
marzipan	小杏仁餅 síu hahng yàhn béng
mayonnaise	沙律醬 sā léut jeung
meat	肉 yuhk
melon	瓜 gwā
meringue	蛋白甜餅 dáan baahk tìhm béng
milk	牛奶 ngàuh náaih
milk shake	奶昔 náaih sīk
mint	薄荷 bohk hòh
monkfish	扁鯊 bín sā
mushroom	蘑菇 mòh gū
mussel	青口 chēng háu
mustard	芥辣 gaai laaht
mutton	羊肉 yèuhng yuhk
noodle	麵 mihn
nori (a type of seaweed)	紫菜 jí choi
nougat	牛奶糖 ngàuh náaih tóng
nutmeg	豆蔻 dauh kau
nuts	硬殼果 ngaahng hok gwó
octopus	章魚 jēung yùh
olive	橄欖 gaam láam
olive oil	橄欖油 gaam láam yàuh
omelet	菴列 ngām liht

onion	蔥 chūng
orange	橙 cháang
orange liqueur	甜橙酒 tìhm cháang jáu
organ meat [offal]	雜碎 jaahp seui
ox	黄牛肉 wòhng ngàuh yuhk
oxtail	牛尾 ngàuh méih
oyster	蠔 hòuh
pancake	薄煎餅 bohk jīn béng
papaya	木瓜 muhk gwā
paprika	辣椒粉 laaht jīu fán
pastry	酥皮點心 sōu péi dím sām
peach	桃 tóu
peanut	花生 fā sāng
pear	梨 léi
peas	豌豆 wún dáu
pecan	合桃 hahp tòuh
pepper (seasoning)	胡椒 wùh jīu
pepper (vegetable)	辣椒 laaht jīu
pheasant	野雞 yéh gāi
pickle	泡菜 paau choi
pie	餅 béng
pineapple	菠蘿 bō lòh
pizza	比薩 pī sàh
plum	李 léih
pomegranate	石榴 sehk láu
pork	豬肉 jyū yuhk
port	缽酒 būt jáu
potato	薯仔 syùh jái

potato chips [crisps]	薯片 syùh pín
prune	梅 múi
pumpkin	南瓜 nàahm gwā
quail	鵪鶉 ngām chēun
rabbit	兔仔肉 tou jái yuhk
radish	蘿蔔 lòh baahk
raisin	提子乾 tàih jí gōn
red bayberry	楊梅 yèuhng múi
red cabbage	紅葉椰菜 hùhng yihp yèh choi
relish	調味品 tìuh meih bán
rice	米 máih
roast	燒 sīu
roast beef	烤牛肉 hāau ngàuh yuhk
roll	卷 gyún
rum	林酒 lām jáu
salad	沙律 sā léut
salami	沙樂美腸 sā lohk méih chéung
salmon	三文魚 sāam màhn yú
salt	鹽 yìhm
sandwich	三文治 sāam màhn jih
sardine	沙甸魚 sā đīn yú
sauce	調味汁 tìuh meih jāp
sausage	香腸 hēung chéung
scallion [spring onion]	大蔥 daaih syun
scallop	扇貝 sin bui
scotch	蘇格蘭威士忌 sōu gaak làahn wāi sih géi
sea bass	鱸魚 lòuh yú
sea perch	中國花鱸 jūng gwok fā lòuh

seafood	海鮮 hói sīn
seaweed	海帶 hói daai
shallot	蔥 chūng
shank	小腿肉 síu téui yuhk
shellfish	貝類 bui leuih
sherry	些利酒 sē leih jáu
shrimp	蝦 hā
silver carp	鰱魚 lìhn yú
sirloin	牛腩 ngàuh náahm
snack	小食 síu sihk
snail	蝸牛 wō ngàuh
soda	蘇打水 sō dá séui
sole	板魚 báan yú
soup	湯 tōng
sour cream	酸奶油 syūn náaih yàuh
soy [soya]	大豆 daaih dáu
soy sauce	豉油 sih yàuh
soybean [soya bean]	大豆 daaih dáu
soymilk [soya milk]	豆奶 dauh náaih
spaghetti	意大利粉 yi daaih leih fán
spices	香料 hēung líu
spinach	菠菜 bō choi
spirits	酒 jáu
squash	南瓜 nàahm gwā
squid	烏賊 wū chaak
steak	牛扒 ngàuh pá
strawberry	士多啤厘 sih dō bē léi

suckling pig	乳豬 yúh jyū
sugar	糖 tòhng
sweet and sour sauce	甜酸醬 tìhm syūn jeung
sweet corn	粟米 sūk mái
sweet pepper	甜椒 tìhm jīu
sweet potato	番薯 fāan syú
sweetener	糖精 tòhng jīng
sweets	糖 tóng
swordfish	劍魚 gim yú
syrup	糖漿 tòhng jēung
tea	茶 chàh
thyme	麝香草 seh hēung chóu
tofu	豆腐 dauh fuh
toast	多士 dō sí
tomato	蕃茄 fāan ké
tongue	舌 sit
tripe	肚 tóuh
trout	鱒魚 jēung yú
truffles	菌 kwán
tuna	金槍魚 gām chōng yú
turkey	火雞 fó gāi
turnip	白蘿蔔 baahk lòh baahk
vanilla	雲尼拿 wahn nēi ná
veal	牛肉 ngàuh yuhk
vegetable	菜 choi
venison	鹿肉 luhk yuhk
vermouth	苦艾酒 fú ngaaih jáu

vinegar	醋 chou
vodka	伏特加 fuhk dahk gā
walnut	合桃 hahp tòuh
water	水 séui
watermelon	西瓜 sāi gwā
wheat	麵粉 mihn fán
whisky	威士忌 wāi sih géi
wine	葡萄酒 pòuh tòuh jáu
yogurt	乳酪 yúh lohk

▼ *People*

Talking

Essential

Hello!	你好! néih hóu
How are you?	你好嗎? néih hóu ma
Fine, thanks.	好好，多謝。hóu hóu dō jeh
Excuse me!	唔該! m gōi
Do you speak English?	你講唔講英文? néih góng m góng yīng màhn
What's your name?	你叫乜野名? néih giu māt yéh méng
My name is…	我叫… ngóh giu…
Nice to meet you.	好高興見到你。hóu gōu hing gin dóu néih
Where are you from?	你喺邊度嚟? néih hái bīn douh làih
I'm from the *U.S./U.K.*	我喺美國/英國嚟。ngóh hái *méih gwok/ yīng gwok* làih
What do you do?	你做乜野工作? néih jouh māt yéh gūng jok
I work for…	我喺…做野 ngóh hái…jouh yéh
I'm a student.	我係學生。ngóh haih hohk sāang
I'm retired.	我退咗休。ngóh teui jó yāu
Do you like…?	你想…? néih séung…
Goodbye.	再見。joi gin

It is polite to address people with: 先生 **sin sāang** (Sir), 女士 **néuih sih** (Madam) or 小姐 **síu jé** (Miss). The Chinese give special respect to older men and women by addressing them with 哥哥 **gòh gō** and 姐姐 **jèh jē**, respectively.

Communication Difficulties

Do you speak English?	你講唔講英文？	néih góng m góng yīng màhn
Does anyone here speak English?	呢度邊個識講英文？	nī douh bīn go sīk góng yīng màhn
I don't speak Chinese.	我唔識講中文。	ngóh m sīk góng jūng màhn
Can you speak more slowly?	你可唔可以講慢啲？	néih hó m hó yíh góng maahn dī
Can you repeat that?	你可唔可以再講一次？	néih hó m hó yíh joi góng yāt chi
Excuse me?	唔該？	m gōi
What was that?	呢個係乜野？	nī go haih māt yéh
Can you spell it?	你可唔可以串出嚟？	néih hó m hó yíh chyun chēut làih
Please write it down.	唔該你寫低。	m gōi néih sé dāi
Can you translate this into English for me?	你可唔可以將呢個翻譯成英文？	néih hó m hó yíh jēung nī go fāan yihk sìhng yīng màhn
What does *this/that* mean?	呢個/嗰個係乜野意思？	*nī go/gó go* haih māt yéh yi sī
I understand.	我明白喇。	ngóh mìhng baahk la
I don't understand.	我唔明白。	ngóh m mìhng baahk
Do you understand?	你明白未？	néih mìhng baahk meih

You May Hear...

我講少少英文。	ngóh góng síu síu yīng màhn	I only speak a little English.
我唔識講英文。	ngóh m sīk góng yīng màhn	I don't speak English.

Making Friends

Hello!	你好！néih hóu
Good morning.	早晨。jóu sàhn
My name is…	我嘅名係… ngóh ge méng haih…
What's your name?	你叫乜野名？néih giu māt yéh méng
I'd like to introduce you to…	我想同你介紹… ngóh séung tùhng néih gaai siuh…
Pleased to meet you.	好高興見到你。hóu gōu hing gin dóu néih
How are you?	你好嗎？néih hóu ma
Fine, thanks. And you?	好好，多謝。你呢？hóu hóu dō jeh néih nē

 A light, quick handshake is generally an accepted greeting in China. A subtle nod and slight bow are other common greetings. You may also see a person lowering his or her eyes upon meeting someone; this is a gesture of respect.

Travel Talk

I'm here…	我喺呢度… ngóh hái nī douh…
– on business	– 工幹 gūng gon
– on vacation [holiday]	– 度假 douh ga
– studying	– 讀書 duhk syū
I'm staying for…	我要留… ngóh yiu làuh…
I've been here…	我喺呢度已經…喇 ngóh hái nī douh yíh gīng…la
– a day	– 一日 yāt yaht
– a week	– 一個星期 yāt go sīng kèih
– a month	– 一個月 yāt go yuht

▶ For numbers, see page 157.

Where are you from?	你喺邊度嚟? néih hái bīn douh làih
I'm from…	我喺…嚟。 ngóh hái…làih

Relationships

Who are you with?	你同邊個一齊嚟? néih tùhng bīn go yāt chàih làih
I'm here alone.	我一個人嚟嘅。 ngóh yāt go yàhn làih
I'm with my…	我同我嘅…一齊嚟嘅。 ngóh tùhng ngóh ge…yāt chàih làih ge
– husband/wife	– 老公/老婆 lóu gūng/lóuh pòh
– boyfriend/girlfriend	– 男/女朋友 nàahm/néuih pàhng yáuh
– friend/colleague	– 朋友/同事 pàhng yáuh/tùhng sih
When's your birthday?	你嘅生日係幾時? néih ge sāang yaht haih géi sìh
How old are you?	你幾大年紀? néih géi daaih nìhn géi
I'm…	我… ngóh…

▶ For numbers, see page 157.

Are you married?	你結咗婚未？ néih git jó fān meih a
I'm…	我… ngóh…
– single/in a relationship	– 單身/有固定朋友 dāan sān/yáuh gu dihng pàhng yáuh
– engaged/married	– 訂咗婚/結咗婚 dihng jó fān/git jó fān
– divorced/separated	– 離咗婚/分咗居 lèih jó fān/fān jó gēui
– widowed	– 老公♀/老婆♂過咗身 lóuh gūng♀/lóuh pòh ♂gwo jó sān
Do you have *children/ grandchildren*?	你有有細蚊仔/孫仔？ néih yáuh móuh *sai mān jái/syūn jái*

Work and School

What do you do?	你做乜野工作？ néih jouh māt yéh gūng jok
What are you studying?	你學緊乜野？ néih hohk gán māt yéh
I'm studying Chinese.	我學緊中文。 ngóh hohk gán jūng màhn
I…	我… ngóh…
– am a consultant	– 係一個顧問 haih yāt go gu mahn
– am unemployed	– 失咗業 sāt jó yihp
– work at home	– 喺屋企工作 hái ngūk kéi gūng jok
Who do you work for?	你幫邊個工作？ néih bōng bīn go gūng jok
I work for…	我幫…工作。 ngóh bōng…gūng jok
Here's my business card.	呢張係我嘅咭片。 nī jēung haih ngóh ge kāat pín

▶ For business travel, see page 134.

Weather

What's the forecast?	天氣預告點?	tīn hei yuh gou dím
What *beautiful/terrible* weather!	今日天氣真係好/唔好!	gām yaht tīn hei jān haih *hóu/m hóu*
It's...	今日…	gām yaht…
– cool/warm	– 涼/暖	lèuhng/nyúhn
– cold/hot	– 凍/熱	dung/yiht
– rainy/sunny	– 落雨/好天	lohk yúh/hóu tīn
– snowy/icy	– 落雪/有冰	lohk syut/yáuh bīng
Do I need *a jacket/ an umbrella*?	我需唔需要外套/遮?	ngóh sēui m sēui yiu *ngoih tou/jē*

▶ For temperature, see page 164.

Romance

Essential

Would you like to go out for *a drink/ dinner*?	你想唔想出去飲野/食晚飯?	néih séung m séung chēut heui *yám yéh/sihk máahn faahn*
What are your plans for *tonight/ tomorrow*?	今晚/聽日你有乜野計畫?	*gām máahn/ tīng yaht* néih yáuh māt yéh gai waahk
Can I have your number?	可唔可以畀你嘅電話號碼我?	hó m hó yíh béi néih ge dihn wá houh máh ngóh
Can I join you?	我可唔可以加入?	ngóh hó m hó yíh gā yahp
Can I get you a drink?	我可唔可以請你飲野?	ngóh hó m hó yíh chéng néih yám yéh
I *like/love* you.	我鍾意/愛你。	ngóh *jūng yi/ngoi* néih

Making Plans

Would you like to go out for coffee?	你想唔想出去飲咖啡？ néih séung m séung chēut heui yám ga fē
What are your plans for…?	你…有乜野計畫？ néih…yáuh māt yéh gai waahk
– today	– 今日 gām yaht
– tonight	– 今晚 gām máahn
– tomorrow	– 聽日 tīng yaht
– this weekend	– 呢個週末 nī go jāu muht
Where would you like to go?	你想去邊度？ néih séung heui bīn douh
I'd like to go to…	我想去… ngóh séung heui…
Do you like…?	你鍾唔鍾意…？ néih jūng m jūng yi…
Can I have your *number/e-mail?*	可唔可以畀你嘅電話號碼/電郵我？ hó m hó yíh béi néih ge *dihn wá houh máh/dihn yàuh* ngóh

▶ For e-mail and phone, see page 49.

Pick-up [Chat-up] Lines

Can I join you?	我可唔可以加入？ ngóh hó m hó yíh gā yahp
You're very attractive.	你非常靚。 néih fēi sèuhng leng
Let's go somewhere quieter.	我哋去個安靜啲嘅地方啦。 ngóh deih heui go ngōn jihng dī ge deih fōng lā

Accepting and Rejecting

OK.	好。 hóu
Where should we meet?	我哋喺邊度見面？ ngóh deih hái bīn douh gin mihn

| I'll meet you *at the bar/at your hotel*. | 我喺酒吧/你嘅酒店見你。ngóh hái j*áu bī*/néih ge jáu dim gin néih |
| I'll come by at… | 我…探你。ngóh…taam néih |

▶ For time, see page 160.

What is your address?	你嘅地址係乜野？néih ge deih jí haih māt yéh
Can we make it *earlier/later*?	我哋可唔可以早/夜啲？ngóh deih hó m hó yíh *jóu/yeh* dī
How about another time?	第二個時間好唔好？daih yih go sìh gaan hóu m hóu
I'm busy.	我好忙。ngóh hóu mòhng
I'm not interested.	我冇興趣。ngóh móuh hing cheui
Leave me alone.	我一個人得喇。ngóh yāt go yàhn dāk la
Stop bothering me!	唔使理我！m sái léih ngóh

Getting Physical

Can I *hug/kiss* you?	我可唔可以攬住/錫你？ngóh hó m hó yíh *láam jyuh/sek* néih
Yes.	得。dāk
No.	唔得。m dāk
I *like/love* you.	我鍾意/愛你。ngóh *jūng yi/ngoih* néih
Stop!	停！tìhng

The Chinese are generally reserved and may not be comfortable when asked forward questions regarding romance or sexuality.

Sexual Preferences

Are you gay?	你係唔係男同性戀者？ néih haih m haih nàahm tùhng sing lyún jé
I'm…	我係… ngóh haih…
– heterosexual	– 異性戀 yih sing lyún
– homosexual	– 同性戀 tùhng sing lyún
– bisexual	– 雙性戀者 sēung sing lyún jé
Do you like *men/ women*?	你鍾唔鍾意男人/女人？ néih jūng m jūng yi *nàahm yán/néuih yán*
Let's go to a gay bar.	我哋去一間基吧啦。 ngóh deih heui yāt gāan gēi bā lā

 Chinese attitudes regarding homosexuality are conservative; therefore, asking about a person's sexuality may not be an appropriate question. Drawing attention to one's sexual orientation is generally discouraged.

The gay community in major Chinese cities is growing, though. Larger cities in China may have gay-friendly bars and clubs but often in discreet locations.

▼ Fun

Sightseeing

Essential

Where's the tourist information office?	旅遊資訊辦公室喺邊度? léuih yàuh jī seun baahn gūng sāt hái bīn douh
What are the main attractions?	主要景點係乜野? jyú yiu gíng dím haih māt yéh
Do you have tours in English?	有冇英文導遊? yáuh móuh yīng màhn douh yàuh
Can I have a *map/ guide*?	我可唔可以要一張地圖/旅遊指南? ngóh hó m hó yíh yiu yāt jēung *deih tòuh/léuih yàuh jí nàahm*

Tourist Information Office

Do you have information on...?	你有冇…嘅資訊? néih yáuh móuh...ge jī seun
How do we get there?	我哋點去嗰度? ngóh deih dím heui gó douh
Can you recommend...?	你可唔可以介紹…? néih hó m hó yíh gaai siuh...
– a bus tour	– 巴士遊覽 bā sí yàuh láahm
– an excursion to...	– 去…遊覽 heui...yàuh láahm
– a sightseeing tour	– 觀光遊覽 gūn gwōng yàuh láahm

Visit a travel agency while in China for tourist information. Agencies that often cater to foreigners include China Travel Services (CTS) and China International Travel Service (CITS); the latter has branches throughout China. Such agencies offer a variety of services (not at all locations): arranging tours; reserving accommodations; providing tickets for trains, operas, acrobatic performances, concerts and more.

Small-scale tour operators can also be of assistance; be sure that the tour operator is licensed before requesting any service.

Tours

I'd like to go on the tour to…	我想去…遊覽。ngóh séung heui…yàuh láahm
When's the next tour?	下一團幾時？hah yāt tyùhn géi sìh
Are there tours in English?	有冇英文導遊？yáuh móuh yīng màhn douh yàuh
Is there an English *guide book/audio guide*?	有冇英文嘅旅遊手冊/錄音旅遊指南？yáuh móuh yīng màhn ge *léuih yàuh sáu chaak/luhk yām léuih yàuh jí nàahm*
What time do we *leave/return*?	我哋幾時出發/返嚟？ngóh deih géi sìh *chēut faat/fāan làih*
We'd like to see…	我哋想睇睇…ngóh deih séung tái tái…
Can we stop here…?	我哋可唔可以停喺呢度…？ngóh deih hó m hó yíh tìhng hái nī douh…
– to take photos	– 影相 yíng séung
– for souvenirs	– 買紀念品 máaih gei nihm bán
– for the restrooms [toilets]	– 去洗手間 heui sái sáu gāan
Is it handicapped [disabled]-accessible?	殘疾人可唔可以用？chàahn jiht yàhn hó m hó yíh yuhng

▶ For ticketing, see page 21.

Sights

Where *is/are*…?	…喺邊度？…hái bīn douh
– the battleground	– 戰場 jin chèuhng
– the botanical garden	– 植物公園 jihk maht gūng yún

105

Where *is/are*...?	···喺邊度？ ...hái bīn douh
– city hall	– 市政大廳 síh jing daaih tēng
– the downtown area	– 市中心 síh jūng sām
– the fountain	– 噴水池 pan séui chìh
– the city hall	– 大會堂 daaih wuih tòhng
– the library	– 圖書館 tòuh syū gún
– the market	– 商場 sēung chèuhng
– the (war) memorial	– （戰爭）紀念館 (jin jāng) gei nihm gún
– the museum	– 博物館 bohk maht gún
– the old town	– 古鎮 gú jan
– the opera house	– 歌劇院 gō kehk yún
– the palace	– 宮殿 gūng dihn
– the park	– 公園 gūng yún
– the ruins	– 遺跡 wàih jīk
– the shopping area	– 購物區 kau maht kēui
Can you show me on the map?	你可唔可以喺地圖上面指畀我睇？ néih hó m hó yíh hái deih tòuh seuhng mihn jí béi ngóh tái

| Is it handicapped [disabled] accessible? | 殘疾人可唔可以用？chàahn jaht yàhn hó m hó yíh yuhng |

▶ For directions, see page 35.

i

Sights in China not to be missed include: the Great Wall, Imperial Palace, Summer Palace, Temple of Heaven, Ming tombs, Xi'an terracotta warriors and so much more. Temples, gardens and other sights can be found in even the smallest towns. For local sights, check with your hotel concierge or a nearby travel agency. Sights are listed on town maps, which can be purchased at newsstands and from street vendors.

There is much to see in China and, after a day filled with sightseeing, you may wish to enjoy some quality entertainment: concerts, acrobatics, Chinese ballet and opera. Of these, a not-to-be-missed event is the Canton opera, a spectacular combination of song, dance, pantomime and martial arts.

Impressions

It's…	好… hóu…
– amazing	– 犀利 sāi leih
– beautiful	– 靚 leng
– boring	– 悶 muhn
– interesting	– 有意思 yáuh yi sī
– magnificent	– 壯觀 jong gūn
– romantic	– 浪漫 lohng maahn
– strange	– 奇怪 kèih gwaai
– stunning	– 令人震驚 lihng yàhn jan gīng
– terrible	– 可怕 hó pa
– ugly	– 難睇 nàahn tái
I (don't) like it.	我（唔）鍾意。ngóh (m) jūng yi

Religion

Where's...?	⋯喺邊度？ ...hái bīn douh
– the *Catholic/ Protestant* church	– 天主教/新教徒教堂 *tīn jyú gaau/sān gaau tòuh* gaau tóng
– the mosque	– 清真寺 chīng jan jí
– the shrine	– 神殿 sàhn dihn
– the synagogue	– 猶太教堂 yàuh taai gaau tòhng
– the temple	– 寺廟 jih míu
What time is *mass/ the service*?	彌撒/禮拜係幾時？ *nèih saat/láih baai* haih géi sìh

i

The People's Republic of China officially subscribes to atheism but, since China's reform, open religious activity has been permitted. Buddhism is the most widely practiced religion in China; Taoism, Islam and Christianity are also observed.

Religion in Hong Kong and Macau is not suppressed. You can find churches and temples in major areas.

Shopping

Essential

Where's the *market/ mall [shopping centre]*?	街市/購物中心喺邊度？ *gāai síh/kau maht jūng sām* hái bīn douh
I'm just looking.	我淨係睇吓。ngóh jihng haih tái háh
Can you help me?	你可唔可以幫我？néih hó m̀ hó yíh bōng ngóh
I'm being helped.	有人幫我喇。yáuh yàhn bōng ngóh la

How much?	幾多錢? géi dō chín
That one, please.	唔該畀嗰個我。 m gōi béi gó go ngóh
That's all.	就呢啲。 jauh nī dī
Where can I pay?	我喺邊度畀錢? ngóh hái bīn douh béi chín
I'll pay *in cash/by credit card*.	我用現金/信用卡畀錢。 ngóh yuhng *yihn gām/seun yuhng kāat* béi chín
A receipt, please.	唔該畀收據我。 m gōi béi sāu geui ngóh

Stores

Where's...?	…喺邊度? ...hái bīn douh
– the antiques store	– 古董店 gú dúng dim
– the bakery	– 麵包舖 mihn bāau póu
– the bank	– 銀行 ngàhn hòhng
– the bookstore	– 書店 syū dim
– the camera store	– 相機鋪 séung gēi póu
– the clothing store	– 時裝店 sìh jōng dim
– the delicatessen	– 熟食店 suhk sihk dim
– the department store	– 百貨公司 baak fo gūng sī
– the gift shop	– 禮品店 láih bán dim
– the health food store	– 健康食品店 gihn hōng sihk bán dim
– the jeweler	– 珠寶店 jyū bóu dim
– the liquor store [off-licence]	– 洋酒店 yèuhng jáu dim
– the mall [shopping centre]	– 購物中心 kau maht jūng sām
– the market	– 街市 gāai síh
– the music store	– 音樂商店 yām ngohk sēung dim

Where's...?	···喺邊度？ ...hái bīn douh
– the pastry shop	– 麵包點心店 mihn bāau dím sām dim
– the pharmacy [chemist]	– 藥房 yeuhk fòhng
– the produce [grocery] store	– 食品店 sihk bán dim
– the shoe store	– 鞋鋪 hàaih póu
– the souvenir store	– 紀念品商店 gei nihm bán sēung dim
– the supermarket	– 超級市場 chīu kāp síh chèuhng
– the toy store	– 玩具鋪 wuhn geuih póu

i Department stores often sell quality goods produced for export and offer a nice selection of souvenirs. Some department stores can send purchases abroad.

Services

Can you recommend...?	你可唔可以介紹…？ néih hó m hó yíh gaai siuh...
– a barber	– 一位理髮師 yāt wái léih faat sī
– a dry cleaner	– 一間乾洗店 yāt gāan gōn sái dim
– a hairstylist	– 一位髮型師 yāt wái faat yìhng sī
– a laundromat [launderette]	– 一間洗衣鋪 yāt gāan sái yī póu
– a spa	– 一間溫泉 yāt gāan wān chyùhn
– a travel agency	– 一間旅行社 yāt gāan léui hàhng séh
Can you...this?	你可唔可以…呢個？ néih hó m hó yíh... nī go
– alter	– 改 gói
– clean	– 洗 sái
– fix [mend]	– 整 jíng
– press	– 熨 tong
When will it be ready?	幾時做完？ géi sìh jouh yùhn

Spa

I'd like...	我想… ngóh séung...
– a facial	– 做面部美容 jouh mihn bouh méih yùhng
– a *manicure/pedicure*	– 修手甲/腳甲 sāu sáu gaap/geuk gaap
– a massage	– 要按摩 yiu ngon mō
Do you do...?	你做唔做…？ néih jouh m jouh...
– acupuncture	– 針灸 jām gau
– aromatherapy	– 香薰療法 hēung fān lìuh faat
– oxygen treatment	– 氧氣治療 yéuhng hei jih lìuh
Do you have a sauna?	你做唔做桑拿？ néih jouh m jouh sōng nàh

Hair Salon

I'd like…	我想… ngóh séung…
– an appointment for *today/tomorrow*	– 約一個今日/聽日嘅時間 yeuk yāt go *gām yaht/tī ng yaht* ge sìh gaan
– some color	– 染髮 yíhm faat
– my hair blow-dried	– 吹頭 chēui tàuh
– a haircut	– 剪頭髮 jín tàuh faat
– a trim	– 剪髮 jín faat
Not too short.	唔好太短。 m̀ hóu taai dyún
Shorter here.	呢度再短一啲。 nī douh joi dyún yāt dī

Sales Help

When do you *open/close*?	幾點開門/閂門？ géi dím *hōi mùhn/sāan mùhn*
Where's…?	…喺邊度？ …hái bīn douh
– the cashier	– 收銀處 sāu ngán chyu
– the escalator	– 電梯 dihn tāi
– the elevator [lift]	– 電梯 dihn tāi
– the fitting room	– 試身室 si sān sāt
Can you help me?	你可唔可以幫我？ néih hó m̀ hó yíh bōng ngóh
I'm just looking.	我只係睇睇。 ngóh jí haih tái tái

I'm being helped.	已經有人幫我喇。 yíh gīng yáuh yàhn bōng ngóh la
Do you have…?	你有冇…? néih yáuh móuh…
Can you show me…?	你可唔可以畀…我睇睇? néih hó m hó yíh béi…ngóh tái tái
Can you *ship/wrap* it?	你可唔可以將呢啲野托運/打包? nèih hó m hó yíh jēung nī dī yéh *tok wahn/dá bāau*
How much?	幾多錢? géi dō chín
That's all.	就呢啲。 jauh nī dī

▶ For clothing items, see page 120.

▶ For food items, see page 82.

▶ For souvenirs, see page 116.

You May Hear…

我可唔可以幫你? ngóh hó m hó yíh bōng néih	Can I help you?
唔該等一等。 m gōi dáng yāt dáng	One moment.
你要乜野? néih yiu māt yéh	What would you like?
仲要唔要第二啲? juhng yiu m yiu daih yih dī	Anything else?

You May See…

開門 hōi mùhn	open
閂門 sāan mùhn	closed
午飯時間關門 ngh faahn sìh gaan gwāan mùhn	closed for lunch
試身室 si sān sāt	fitting room
付款處 fuh fún chyu	cashier
只收現金 jí sāu yihn gām	cash only
接受信用卡 jip sauh seun yuhng kāat	credit cards accepted

113

| 營業時間 yìhng yihp sìh gaan | business hours |
| 出口 chēut háu | exit |

Preferences

I'd like something…	我想要… ngóh séung yiu…
– cheap/expensive	– 平啲/貴啲嘅 *pèhng dī/gwai dī* ge
– larger/smaller	– 大啲/細啲嘅 *daaih dī/sai dī* ge
– nicer	– 好啲嘅 hóu dī ge
– from this region	– 當地生產嘅 dōng deih sāng cháan ge
Around…Hong Kong dollars.	…蚊左右嘅。 …mān jó yáu ge
Is it real?	呢啲係唔係真嘅? nī dī haih m haih jān ge
Can you show me *this/that*?	你可唔可以畀我睇吓個/嗰個? néih hó m hó yíh béi ngóh tái háh *nī go/gó go*

Decisions

That's not quite what I want.	嗰個唔係我要嘅。 gó go m haih ngóh yiu ge
No, I don't like it.	我唔鍾意。 ngóh m jūng yi
It's too expensive.	太貴喇。 taai gwai la
I have to think about it.	我要諗諗。 ngóh yiu nám nám
I'll take it.	我要。 ngóh yiu

Bargaining

That's too much.	太貴喇。 taai gwai la
I'll give you…	我畀…你。 ngóh béi…néih
I have only…Hong Kong dollars.	我只有…港幣。 ngóh jí yáuh…góng baih

| Is that your best price? | 係唔係最低價？ haih m haih jeui dāi ga |
| Can you give me a discount? | 可唔可以打折？ hó m hó yíh dá jit |

▶ For numbers, see page 157.

Paying

How much?	幾多錢？ géi dō chín
I'll pay…	我要用…畀錢。 ngóh yiu yuhng…béi chín
– in cash	– 現金 yihn gām
– by credit card	– 信用卡 seun yuhng kāat
– by traveler's check [cheque]	– 旅行支票 léuih hàhng jī piu
Can I use this…?	我可唔可以用…卡？ ngóh hó m hó yíh yuhng…kāat
– ATM	– 自動提款機 jih duhng tàih fún gēi
– credit	– 信用 seun yuhng
– gift	– 禮品 láih bán
How do I use this machine?	呢架機器點樣用？ nī ga gēi hei dím yéung yuhng
A receipt, please.	唔該畀收據我。 m gōi béi sāu geui ngóh

You May Hear…

你點樣畀錢？ néih dím yéung béi chín	How are you paying?
你嘅信用卡被拒絕。 néih ge seun yuhng kāat beih kéuih jyuht	Your credit card has been declined.
唔該出示你嘅身份證。 m gōi chēut sih néih ge sān fán jing	ID, please.
我哋唔接受信用卡。 ngóh deih m jip sauh seun yuhng kāat	We don't accept credit cards.
唔該畀現金。 m gōi béi yihn gām	Cash only, please.

115

In Hong Kong and throughout China, the most commonly accepted form of payment is cash. Major credit cards may be accepted at larger stores in city centers.

Complaints

I'd like…	我想… ngóh séung…
– to exchange this	– 換一個 wuhn yāt go
– a refund	– 退款 teui fún
– to see the manager	– 見經理 gin gīng léih

Souvenirs

book	書 syū
box of chocolates	朱古力 jyū gū līk
calligraphy supplies	書法用品 syū faat yuhng bán
Chinese painting	中國畫 jūng gwok wá
chopsticks	筷子 faai jí
cloisonné	景泰藍 gíng taai làahm
doll	公仔 gūng jái
jade	玉 yúk
key ring	鑰匙扣 só sìh kau
lacquerware	漆器 chāt hei
porcelain	瓷器 chìh hei
postcard	明信片 mìhng seun pín
pottery	瓷器 chìh hei
silk	絲綢 sī chàuh
T-shirt	T恤 tī sēut
toy	玩具 wuhn geuih

Can I see *this/that*?	我可唔可以睇睇呢個/嗰個？ ngóh hó m hó yíh tái tái *nī go/gó go*
It's in the *window/ display case*.	喺櫥窗/陳列櫃裏面。hái *chyùh chēung/ chàhn liht gwaih* léuih mihn
I'd like…	我想要… ngóh séung yiu…
– a battery	– 一個電芯 yāt go dihn sām
– a bracelet	– 一隻手扼 yāt jek sáu ngáak
– a brooch	– 一個心口針 yāt go sām háu jām
– a clock	– 一個鐘 yāt go jūng
– earrings	– 一對耳環 yāt deui yíh wáan
– a necklace	– 一條頸鏈 yāt tìuh géng lín
– a ring	– 一隻戒指 yāt jek gaai jí
– a watch	– 一個手錶 yāt go sáu bīu
I'd like…	我想要…嘅。ngóh séung yiu…ge
– copper	– 銅 tùhng
– crystal	– 水晶 séui jīng
– diamonds	– 鑽石 jyun sehk
– *white/yellow* gold	– 白/黃金 *baahk/wòhng* gām

117

I'd like…	我想要…嘅。ngóh séung yiu…ge
– pearls	– 珍珠 jān jyū
– platinum	– 鉑金 baahk gām
– sterling silver	– 純銀 sèuhn ngán
Is this real?	呢啲係唔係真嘅？nī dī haih m haih jān ge
Can you engrave it?	你可唔可以喺上面刻字？néih hó m hó yíh hái seuhng mihn hāk jih

i

Typical Chinese souvenirs include silk fabric and clothing, jade, pearls and porcelain. Jade is traditionally worn for good luck, as a protection against illness and as an amulet for travelers. Pearls are also part of Chinese tradition; they have been worn by emperors and other nobility. Calligraphy supplies, kites, paper cuts and chopsticks are also popular mementos. Souvenirs can be found in malls, department stores and local street markets.

If you're antiquing, note that items dated earlier than 1795 may not be legally exported; any antique leaving China must be affixed with a small red seal, provided by the Cultural Relics Bureau.

Antiques

How old is it?	有幾長歷史？yáuh géi chèuhng lihk sí
Do you have anything from the…period?	你有冇…時期嘅野？néih yáuh móuh… sìh kèih ge yéh
Do I have to fill out any forms?	我使唔使填表？ngóh sái m sái tìhn bíu
Is there a certificate of authenticity?	有冇真品證明？yáuh móuh jān bán jing mìhng

Clothing

I'd like…	我想要… ngóh séung yiu…
Can I try this on?	我可唔可以試著？ ngóh hó m hó yíh si jeuk
It doesn't fit.	唔適合。 m sīk hahp
It's too…	太… taai…
– big/small	– 大/細 daaih/sai
– short/long	– 短/長 dyún/chèuhng
– tight/loose	– 緊/闊 gán/fut
Do you have this in size…?	呢件衫有冇…號嘅？ nī gihn sāam yáuh móuh…houh ge
Do you have this in a *bigger/smaller* size?	呢件衫有冇大/細啲嘅嗎？ nī gihn sāam yáuh móuh *daaih/sai* dī ge

▶ For numbers, see page 157.

You May Hear...

嗰件衫好適合你。 nī gihn sāam hóu sīk hahp néih	That looks great on you.
適唔適合我？ sīk m sīk hahp ngóh	How does it fit?
我哋冇你嘅尺寸。 ngóh deih móuh néih ge chek chyun	We don't have your size.

Clothing—Western and traditional Chinese—is sold at street markets and local department stores, usually at very reasonable prices. Designer clothing is available at high-end boutiques, found in larger cities. China is known for its silk production, and silk clothing and fabric (by the yard) can be purchased in many stores.

男士嘅 nàahm sih ge	men's
女士嘅 néuih sih ge	women's
細蚊仔嘅 sai mān jái ge	children's

Color

I'd like something… 我想要… ngóh séung yiu…	
– beige	– 米黃 máih wòhng
– black	– 黑色 hāak sīk
– blue	– 藍色 làahm sīk
– brown	– 咖啡色 ga fē sīk
– gray	– 灰色 fūi sīk
– green	– 綠色 luhk sīk
– orange	– 橙色 cháang sīk
– pink	– 粉紅色 fán hùhng sīk
– purple	– 紫色 jí sīk
– red	– 紅色 hùhng sīk
– white	– 白色 baahk sīk
– yellow	– 黃色 wòhng sīk

Clothes and Accessories

backpack	背囊 bui nòhng
belt	皮帶 pèih dáai
bikini	比基尼 béi gīn nèih
blouse	女裝恤衫 néuih jōng sēut sāam
bra	胸圍 hūng wàih
briefs [underpants]	底褲 dái fu

coat	外套 ngoih tou
dress	禮服 láih fuhk
hat	帽 móu
jacket	褸 lāu
jeans	牛仔褲 ngàuh jái fu
pajamas	睡衣 seuih yī
pants [trousers]	長褲 chèuhng fu
pantyhose [tights]	絲襪 sī maht
purse [handbag]	女裝銀包 néuih jōng ngàhn bāau
raincoat	雨褸 yúh lāu
scarf	絲巾 sī gān
shirt	恤衫 sēut sām
shorts	短褲 dyún fu
skirt	裙 kwàhn
socks	襪 maht
suit	套裝 tou jōng
sunglasses	太陽眼鏡 taai yèuhng ngáhn géng
sweater	毛衫 mòuh sāam
sweatshirt	運動衫 wahn duhng sāam
swimsuit	泳衣 wihng yī
T-shirt	T恤 tī sēut
tie	領呔 léhng tāai
underwear	底衫 dái sāam

Fabric

I'd like…	我想要… ngóh séung yiu…
– cotton	– 棉布 mìhn bou
– denim	– 粗棉布 chōu mìhn bou

I'd like…	我想要… ngóh séung yiu…
– lace	– 花邊 fā bīn
– leather	– 皮 péi
– linen	– 麻布 màh bou
– silk	– 絲綢 sī chàuh
– wool	– 羊毛 yèuhng mòuh
Is it machine washable?	可唔可以機洗？ hó m hó yíh gēi sái

Shoes

I'd like…	我想要… ngóh séung yiu…
– high-heels/flats	– 高挣鞋/平底鞋 gōu jāang hàaih/pìhng dái hàaih
– boots	– 靴 hēu
– loafers	– 平底便服鞋 pìhng dái bihn fuhk hàaih
– sandals	– 涼鞋 lèuhng hàaih
– shoes	– 鞋 hàaih
– slippers	– 拖鞋 tō háai
– sneakers	– 運動鞋 wahn duhng hàaih
In size…	…號 …houh

▶ For numbers, see page 157.

In department stores and places where clothes are made for export, sizes will be given as small, medium and large. Most other clothing stores feature Chinese measurements that combine height and chest size; these measurements appear in centimeters. For example, if you are 170 cm tall (5'6") with a chest measurement of 90 cm (36"), look for clothing marked 170/90. Children's sizes are given by height, in centimeters.

Sizes

chest measurement	胸圍 hūng wàih
waist measurement	腰圍 yīu wàih
height	身長 sān chèuhng
extra small	加細碼 gā sai máh
small	細碼 sai máh
medium	中碼 jūng máh
large	大碼 daaih máh
extra large	加大碼 gā daaih máh
plus size	加加大碼 gā gā daaih máh

Newsstand and Tobacconist

Do you sell English-language newspapers?	你賣唔賣英文報紙？néih maaih m maaih yīng màhn bou jí
I'd like…	我想買… ngóh séung máaih…
– a cigar	– 雪茄 syut kā
– a *pack/carton* of cigarettes	– 一包/一條煙 yāt bāau/yāt tìuh yīn
– a lighter	– 一個打火機 yāt go dá fó gēi
I'd like…	我想買… ngóh séung máaih…
– a magazine	– 一本雜誌 yāt bún jaahp ji
– matches	– 火柴 fó chàaih
– a newspaper	– 一份報紙 yāt fahn bou jí
– a phone card	– 一張電話卡 yāt jēung dihn wá kāat
– a postcard	– 一張明信片 yāt jēung mìhn seun pín
– a *road/town* map of…	– …道路/市區地圖 …douh louh/síh kēui deih tòuh
– stamps	– 郵票 yàuh piu

Photography

I'd like…camera.	我想買一個…相機。 ngóh séung máaih yāt go…séung gēi
– an automatic	– 自動 jih duhng
– a digital	– 數碼 sou máh
– a disposable	– 即棄 jīk hei
I'd like…	我想… ngóh séung…
– a battery	– 買一個電芯 máaih yāt go dihn sām
– digital prints	– 數碼列印照片 sou máh liht yan jiu pín
– a memory card	– 買存儲卡 máaih chyúh jihk kaat
Can I print digital photos here?	我可唔可以喺呢度列印數碼照片？ ngóh hó m hó yíh hái nī douh liht yan sou máh jiu pín

Sports and Leisure

Essential

When's the game?	幾時比賽？ géi sìh béi choi
Where's…?	…喺邊度？ …hái bīn douh
– the beach	– 海灘 hói tāan
– the park	– 公園 gūng yún

– the pool	– 泳池 wihng chìh
Is it safe to swim here?	喺呢度游水安唔安全？ hái nī douh yàuh séui ngōn m ngōn chyùhn
Can I rent [hire] golf clubs?	可唔可以租棒球？ hó m hó yíh jōu kàuh páahng
How much per hour?	每個鐘頭幾多錢？ múih go jūng tàuh géi dō chín
How far is it to…?	去…有幾遠？ heui…yáuh géi yúhn
Show me on the map, please.	唔該喺地圖上面指畀我睇。 m gōi hái deih tòuh seuhng mihn jí béi ngóh tái

Spectator Sports

When's…*game/match*?	…比賽係幾時？ …béi choi haih géi sìh
– the baseball	– 棒球 páahng kàuh
– the basketball	– 籃球 làahm kàuh
– the golf	– 高爾夫球 gōu yíh fū kàuh
– the badminton	– 羽毛球 yúh mòuh kàuh
– the ping-pong	– 乒乓波 bīng bām bō
– the martial arts	– 武術 móuh seuht
– the soccer [football]	– 足球 jūk kàuh
– the tennis	– 網球 móhng kàuh
– the volleyball	– 排球 pàaih kàuh
– the wrestling	– 摔跤 sēut gāau
Who's playing?	邊個打緊波？ bīn go dá gán bō
Where's the *racetrack/stadium*?	跑馬場/體育場喺邊度？ páau máh chèuhng/wahn duhng chèuhng hái bīn douh

▶ For ticketing, see page 21.

ℹ️ Early risers will no doubt encounter people practicing taichi (太極 **taai gihk**), a combination of martial arts and relaxation movements, in parks throughout China. Some also practice qigong (氣功 **hei gūng**), breathing and movement exercises. If you are interested in joining, the crowd would welcome you!

Other sports enjoyed in China include badminton and ping-pong. Volleyball courts and swimming pools can be found throughout China. If you're looking for brain exercise instead of a body stretch, try mahjong (麻雀 **màh jeuk**), a popular Chinese strategy game. Chinese chess and cards are common as well.

Participating

Where *is/are*...?	…喺邊度？ …hái bīn douh
– the golf course	– 高爾夫球場 gōu yíh fū kàuh chèuhng
– the gym	– 健身房 gihn sān fòhng
– the park	– 公園 gūng yún
– the tennis courts	– 網球場 móhng kàuh chèuhng

How much per…?	每…幾多錢?	múih…géi dō chín
– day	– 日	yaht
– hour	– 個鐘頭	go jūng tàuh
– game	– 場比賽	chèuhng béi choi
– round	– 輪比賽	lèuhn béi choi
Can I rent [hire]…?	我可唔可以租…?	ngóh hó m hó yíh jōu…
– clubs	– 球棒	kàuh páahng
– equipment	– 設備	chit beih
– a racket	– 一個球拍	yāt go kàuh paak

At the Beach/Pool

Where's the *beach/pool*?	海灘/泳池喺邊度?	*hói tāan/wìhng chìh* hái bīn douh
Is there…?	有冇…?	yáuh móuh…
– a kiddie pool	– 兒童泳池	yìh tùhng wìhng chìh
– an *indoor/outdoor* pool	– 室內/室外游泳池	*sāt noih/sāt ngoih* yàuh wìhng chìh
– a lifeguard	– 救生員	gau sāng yùhn
Is it safe…?	…安唔安全?	…ngōn m ngōn chyùhn
– to swim	– 游水	yàuh séui
– to dive	– 潛水	chìhm séui
– for children	– 細蚊仔用	sai mān jái yuhng
I'd like to rent [hire]…	我想租…	ngóh séung jōu…
– a deck chair	– 一張接椅	yāt jēung jip yí
– diving equipment	– 一套潛水用具	yāt tou chìhm séui yuhng geuih

I'd like to rent [hire]…	我想租… ngóh séung jōu…
– a jet ski	– 一套噴氣式滑水板 yāt gou pan hei sīk waaht séui báan
– a motorboat	– 一艘汽艇 yāt sáu hei téng
– a rowboat	– 一隻艇仔 yāt jek téng jái
– snorkeling equipment	– 潛水設備 chìhm séui chi beih
– a surfboard	– 一塊滑浪板 yāt faai waaht lohng báan
– a towel	– 一條毛巾 yāt tìuh mòuh gān
– an umbrella	– 一把遮 yāt bá jē
– water skis	– 滑水橇 waaht séui hīu
– a windsurfer	– 一隻帆船 yāt jek fàahn syùhn
For…hours.	一共…個鐘頭。 yāt guhng…go jūng tàuh

Public beaches can be found around Hong Kong and along China's east coast. The most popular beaches are often very crowded, so arrive early for a good spot.

Winter Sports

A ticket for the skating rink, please.	唔該一張溜冰場入場券。 m gōi yāt jēung làuh bīng chèuhng yahp chèuhng hyun
I want to rent [hire] ice skates.	我想租溜冰鞋。 ngóh séung jōu làuh bīng hàaih
Can I take skating lessons?	我可唔可以上溜冰堂。 ngóh hó m hó yíh séung làuh bīg tòhng
I'm a beginner.	我係初學者。 ngóh haih chō hohk jé

Due to year-round warm temperatures, winter sports are generally not popular in Cantonese-speaking China. Skating rinks can be found inside some large shopping malls in Hong Kong.

In the Countryside

A map of…, please.	唔該畀一份…地圖我。 m gōi béi yāt fahn…deih tòuh ngóh
– this region	– 呢個地區嘅 nī go deih kēui ge
– the walking routes	– 步行路線 bouh hàhng louh sin
– the bike routes	– 單車路線 dāan chē louh sin
– the trails	– 行山道 hàahng sāan douh
Is it…?	係唔係…? haih m haih…
– easy	– 容易 yùhng yi
– difficult	– 難 nàahn
– far	– 遠 yúhn
– steep	– 斜 che
I'm exhausted.	我好癐喇。 ngóh hóu guih la
How far is it to…?	離…有幾遠? lèih…yáuh géi yúhn
Show me on the map, please.	唔該喺地圖上面指畀我睇。 m gōi hái deih tòuh seuhng mihn jí béi ngóh tái
I'm lost.	我盪失路。 ngóh dohng sāt louh
Where's…?	…喺邊度? …hái bīn douh
– the bridge	– 橋 kìuh
– the cave	– 洞 duhng
– the cliff	– 懸崖 yùhn ngàaih
– the desert	– 沙漠 sā mohk
– the farm	– 農場 nùhng chèuhng
– the field	– 農田 nùhng tìhn
– the forest	– 森林 sām làhm
– the mountain	– 山 sāan
– the lake	– 湖 wùh
– the nature preserve	– 自然保護區 jih yìhn bóu wuh kēui

Where's...?	···喺邊度？ ...hái bīn douh
– the overlook [viewpoint]	– 觀景點 gūn gíng dím
– the park	– 公園 gūng yún
– the path	– 道路 douh louh
– the peak	– 山頂 sāan déng
– the picnic area	– 野餐區 yéh chāan kēui
– the pond	– 池塘 chìh tóng
– the river	– 河流 hòh làuh
– the sea	– 大海 daaih hói
– the stream	– 小河 síu hòh
– the thermal spring	– 溫泉 wān chyùhn
– the valley	– 山谷 sāan gūk
– the vineyard	– 葡萄園 pòuh tòuh yùhn
– the waterfall	– 瀑布 bohk bou

Culture and Nightlife

Essential

What's there to do at night?	夜晚可以做乜野呢？yeh máahn hó yíh jouh māt yéh nē
Do you have a program of events?	你有冇節目表？néih yáuh móuh jit muhk bíu
What's playing tonight?	今晚做乜野？gām máahn jouh māt yéh
Where's...?	···喺邊度？ ...hái bīn douh
– the downtown area	– 市中心 síh jūng sām
– the bar	– 酒吧 jáu bā

– the dance club	– 跳舞俱樂部 tiu móuh kēui lohk bouh
Is there a cover charge?	有冇附加費？ yáuh móuh fuh gā fai

Entertainment

Can you recommend...?	你可唔可以介紹…？ néih hó m hó yíh gaai siuh...
– a concert	– 一個音樂會 yāt go yām ngohk wúi
– a movie	– 一部電影 yāt bouh dihn yíng
– an opera	– 一部歌劇 yāt bouh gō kehk
– a play	– 一部戲劇 yāt bouh hei kehk
When does it *start/ end*?	幾點開始/結束？ géi dím *hōi chí/git chūk*
Where's...?	…喺邊度？ ...hái bīn douh
– the concert hall	– 音樂廳 yām ngohk tēng
– the opera house	– 歌劇院 gō kehk yún
– the theater	– 劇院 kehk yún
I like...	我鍾意… ngóh jūng yi...
– classical music	– 古典音樂 gú dín yām ngohk
– folk music	– 民族音樂 màhn juhk yām ngohk
– jazz	– 爵士樂 jeuk sih ngohk
– pop music	– 流行音樂 làuh hàhng yām ngohk

▶ For ticketing, see page 21.

You May Hear...

唔該熄手機。 m gōi sīk sáu gēi	**Turn off your cell [mobile] phones, please.**

Nightlife is more common in south China than elsewhere; restaurants, bars and cafes usually stay open until at least midnight in the south. However, Hong Kong, which is known as the pearl of the Orient, is a city with a thriving night scene. Bars and dance clubs can be found in major tourist areas and near hotels. English-language newpapers often list cultural ongoings in major cities. Ask about local events at your hotel or check for events listings in a local newspaper.

Nightlife

What's there to do at night?	夜晚可以做乜野？	yeh máahn hó yíh jouh māt yéh
Can you recommend...?	你可唔可以介紹…？	néih hó m hó yíh gaai siuh...
– a bar	– 一個酒吧	yāt go jáu bā
– a casino	– 一個賭場	yāt go dóu chèuhng
– a dance club	– 跳舞俱樂部	tiu móuh kēui lohk bouh
– a jazz club	– 爵士樂俱樂部	jeuk sih ngohk kēui lohk bouh
– a club with Chinese music	– 一間有中國音樂嘅俱樂部	yāt gāan yáuh jūng gwok yām ngohk ge kēui lohk bouh
Is there live music?	有冇現場音樂？	yáuh móuh yihn chèuhng yām ngohk
How do I get there?	我點樣去嗰度？	ngóh dím heui gó douh
Is there a cover charge?	有冇附加費？	yáuh móuh fuh gā fai
Let's go dancing.	我哋去跳舞啦。	ngóè deih heui tiu móuh lā

Special Needs

Business Travel

Essential

I'm here on business.	我喺呢度工幹。ngóh hái nī douh gūng gon
Here's my business card.	呢張係我嘅咭片。nī jēung haih ngóh ge kāat pín
Can I have your card?	可唔可以畀你嘅咭片我？hó m hó yíh béi néih ge kāat pín ngóh
I have a meeting with…	我同…有一個會。ngóh tùhng…yáuh yāt go wúi
Where's…?	…喺邊度？…hái bīn douh
– the business center	– 商業中心 sēung yihp jūng sām
– the convention hall	– 會議廳 wuih yíh tēng
– the meeting room	– 會議室 wuih yíh sāt

Conducting business in China should be done respectfully. When presenting or receiving a business card in China, be sure to hold the card in both hands. If you have just received a card, do not put it away before reading the card.

Note that Chinese surnames precede given names; therefore, Li Yang should be referred to as Mr Li. Some Chinese professionals have adopted Western first names and name order, though.

Business Communication

I'm here for a *seminar/ conference*.	我喺呢度開研討會/開會 ngóh hái nī douh *hōi yìhn tóu wúi/hōi wúi*
My name is…	我叫… ngóh giu…

May I introduce my colleague…	我介紹一下同事… ngóh gaai siuh yāt háh tùhng sih…
I have *a meeting/an appointment* with…	我同…有一個會/約。ngóh tùhng…yáuh yāt go *wúi/yeuk*
I'm sorry I'm late.	對唔住我遲到。deui m jyuh ngóh chìh dou
I need an interpreter.	我需要翻譯。ngóh sēui yiu fāan yihk
You can reach me at the…Hotel.	你可以喺…酒店搵到我。néih hó yíh hái…jáu dim wán dóu ngóh
I'm here until…	我要喺呢度留到… ngóh yiu hái nī douh làuh dou…
I need to…	我需要… ngóh sēui yiu…
– make a call	– 打電話 dá dihn wá
– make a photocopy	– 影印 yíng yan
– send an e-mail	– 發電郵 faat dihn yàuh
– send a fax	– 發傳真 faat chyùhn jān
– send a package (overnight)	– 寄一個（第二日送到嘅）包裹 gei yāt go (daih yih yaht sung dou ge) bāau gwó
It was a pleasure to meet you.	好高興見到你。hóu gōu hing gin dóu néih

▶ For internet and communications, see page 49.

135

你有冇預約？néih yáuh móuh yuh yeuk	Do you have an appointment?
同邊個？tùhng bīn go	With whom?
佢開緊會。kéuih hōi gán wúi	He/She is in a meeting.
唔該等一等。m gōi dáng yāt dáng	One moment, please.
唔該坐吓。m gōi chóh háh	Have a seat.
你要唔要飲啲乜野？néih yiu m yiu yám dī māt yéh	Would you like something to drink?
多謝光臨。dō jeh gwōng làhm	Thank you for coming.

Travel with Children

Essential

Is there a discount for kids?	細蚊仔有冇折？sai mān jái yáuh móuh jit
Can you recommend a babysitter?	你可唔可以介紹一位保姆？néih hó m hó yíh gaai siuh yāt wái bóu móuh
Do you have a *child's seat/highchair*?	你有冇BB凳/高凳？néih yáuh móuh *bìh bī dang/gōu dang*
Where can I change the baby?	我喺邊度可以幫細蚊仔換尿片？ngó hái bīn douh hó yíh bōng sai mān jái wuhn niuh pín

Fun with Kids

Can you recommend something for kids?	你可唔可以推薦細蚊仔玩嘅活動？néih hó m hó yíh tēui jin sai mān jái wáan ge wuht duhng
Where's…?	…喺邊度？…hái bīn douh
– the amusement park	– 遊樂園 yàuh lohk yùhn
– the kiddie [paddling] pool	– 兒童泳池 yìh tùhng wihng chìh
– the park	– 公園 gūng yún
– the playground	– 操場 chōu chèuhng
– the zoo	– 動物園 duhng maht yùhn
Are kids allowed?	細蚊仔可唔可以入去？sai mān jái hó m hó yíh yahp heui
Is it safe for kids?	細蚊仔玩安唔安全？sai mān jái wáan ngōn m ngōn chyùhn
Is it suitable for… year olds?	適唔適合…歲嘅細蚊仔？sīk m sīk hahp… seui ge sai mān jái

▶ For numbers, see page 157.

You May Hear…

真係可愛！jān haih hó ngoi	How cute!
佢叫乜野名？kéuih giu māt yéh méng	What's his/her name?
佢幾大？kéuih géi daaih	How old is he/she?

Basic Needs for Kids

Do you have…?	你有冇…? néih yáuh móuh…
– a baby bottle	– 奶樽 náaih jēun
– baby food	– 嬰兒食品 yīng yìh sihk bán
– baby wipes	– 嬰兒紙巾 yīng yìh jí gān
– a car seat	– 汽車安全座椅 hei chē ngōn chyùhn yí
– a children's menu	– 兒童菜單 yìh tùhng choi dāan

▶ For dining with kids, see page 63.

– a child's seat/ highchair	– BB凳/高凳 bìh bī dang/gōu dang
– a crib/cot	– 搖籃/床仔 yìuh láam/chòhng jái
– diapers [nappies]	– 尿片 niuh pín
– formula [baby food]	– 奶粉 náaih fán
– a pacifier [soother]]	– 奶嘴 náaih jéui
– a playpen	– 遊戲圍欄 yàuh hei wàih làahn
– a stroller [pushchair]	– BB 車 bìh bī chē
Can I breastfeed the baby here?	我可唔可以喺呢度餵細蚊仔人奶? ngóh hó m hó yíh hái nī douh wai sai mān jái yàhn náaih
Where can I breastfeed/change the baby?	我喺邊度可以餵細蚊仔食人奶/幫細蚊仔換尿片? ngóh hái bīn douh hó yíh wai sai mān jái sihk yàhn náaih/bōng sai mān jái wuhn niuh pín

Babysitting

Can you recommend a babysitter?	你可唔可以介紹一位保姆? néih hó m hó yíh gaai siuh yāt wái bóu móuh
What's the charge?	你哋收費係幾多? néih deih sāu fai haih géi dō

| I'll be back by… | 我喺⋯之前返嚟。ngóh hái…jī chìhn fāan làih |
| I can be reached at… | 打⋯可以搵到我。dá…hó yíh wán dóu ngóh |

Health and Emergency

| Can you recommend a pediatrician? | 你可唔可以介紹一位兒科醫生？néih hó m hó yíh gaai siuh yāt wái yìh fō yī sāng |
| My child is allergic to… | 我嘅細蚊仔對⋯過敏。ngóh ge sai mān jái deui…gwo máhn |

▶ For food items, see page 82.

| My child is missing. | 我嘅細蚊仔唔見咗。ngóh ge sai mān jái m gin jó |
| Have you seen a *boy/girl*? | 你有冇睇到一個男仔/女仔？néih yáuh móuh tái dóu yāt go *nàahm jái/néuih jái* |

▶ For health, see page 145.

▶ For police, see page 143.

For the Disabled

Essential

Is there…?	有冇…? yáuh móuh…
– access for the disabled	– 殘疾人通道 chàahn jaht yàhn tūng douh
– a wheelchair ramp	– 輪椅通道 lèuhn yí tūng douh
– a handicapped-[disabled-] accessible toilet	– 一間殘疾人可以用嘅洗手間 yāt gāan chàahn jaht yàhn hó yíh yuhng ge sái sáu gāan
I need…	我需要… ngóh sēui yiu…
– assistance	– 幫助 bōng joh
– an elevator [a lift]	– 電梯 dihn tāi
– a ground-floor room	– 一間一樓嘅房 yāt gāan yāt láu ge fóng

Getting Help

I'm…	我… ngóh…
– disabled	– 係殘疾人 haih chàahn jaht yàhn
– visually impaired	– 視力唔好 sih lihk m hóu
– hearing impaired/ deaf	– 聽力唔好/耳聾 ting lihk m hóu/yíh lùhng
– unable to *walk far/ use the stairs*	– 唔可以行好遠/行樓梯 m hó yíh *hàahng hóu yúhn/hàahng làuh tāi*

Please speak louder.	唔該大聲講。m gōi daaih sēng góng
Can I bring my wheelchair?	我可唔可以帶輪椅？ngóh m hó yíh daai lèuhn yí
Are guide dogs permitted?	導盲犬可唔可以入？douh màahng hyún hó m hó yíh yahp
Can you help me?	你可唔可以幫我？néih hó m hó yíh bōng ngóh
Please *open/hold* the door.	唔該打開/拉著門。m gōi *dá hōi/lāai jyuh* mùhn

▼ Resources

Emergencies

Essential

Help!	救命! gau mehng
Go away!	走開! jáu hōi
Stop, thief!	唔好走，有賊! m hóu jáu yáuh cháak
Get a doctor!	搵醫生! wán yī sāng
Fire!	著火啦! jeuhk fó la
I'm lost.	我盪失路。 ngóh dohng sāt louh
Can you help me?	你可唔可以幫我? néih hó m hó yíh bōng ngóh

Police

Essential

Call the police!	打電話畀警察! dá dihn wá béi gíng chaat
Where's the police station?	警察局喺邊度? gíng chaat gúk hái bīn douh
There was an *accident/attack*.	有意外/人受襲擊。 yáuh *yi ngoih/yàhn sauh jaahp gīk*
My child is missing.	我嘅細蚊仔唔見咗。 ngóh ge sai mān jái m gin jó
I need...	我需要… ngóh sēui yiu…
– an interpreter	– 一個翻譯 yāt go fāan yihk
– to contact my lawyer	– 聯絡我嘅律師 lyùhn lohk ngóh ge leuht sī
– to make a phone call	– 打電話 dá dihn wá
I'm innocent.	我係無辜嘅。 ngóh haih mouh gū ge

143

You May Hear...

填好呢份表格。	tìhn hóu nī fahn bíu gaak	Fill out this form.
唔該出示你嘅身份證。	m gōi néih chēut sih néih ge sān fán jing	Your identification, please.
係幾時/喺邊度發生?	haih *géi sìh/hái bīn douh* faat sāng	*When/Where* did it happen?
佢點樣?	kéuih dím yéung	What does he/she look like?

i

The emergency number in Hong Kong is 999. This number connects you to the central reporting center and will be then directed to the police, ambulance or fire station.

Elsewhere, the emergency numbers in China are as follows: 110, police; 120, ambulance; 119, fire emergency. A list of important numbers, including local emergency services, should be available at your hotel or the tourist information office.

Lost Property and Theft

I'd like to report...	我想報告一個…事件。 ngóh séung bou gou yāt go...sih gín
– a mugging	– 搶劫 chéung gip
– a rape	– 強姦 kèuhng gāan
– a theft	– 偷竊 tāu sit
I was *mugged/ robbed*.	我畀人搶野/打劫。 ngóh béi yàhn *chéung yéh/dá gip*
I lost my...	我嘅…唔見咗。 ngóh ge...m gin jó
My...was stolen.	我嘅…畀人偷咗。 ngóh ge...béi yàhn tāu jó
– backpack	– 背囊 bui nòhng

– bicycle	– 單車 dāan chē
– camera	– 相機 séung gēi
– (rental [hire]) car	– （租嘅）車 (jōu ge) chē
– computer	– 電腦 dihn nóuh
– credit card	– 信用卡 seun yuhng kāat
– jewelry	– 首飾 sáu sīk
– money	– 錢 chín
– passport	– 護照 wuh jiu
– purse [handbag]	– 銀包 ngàhn bāau
– traveler's checks [cheques]	– 旅行支票 léuih hàhng jī piu
– wallet	– 銀包 ngàhn bāau
I need a police report.	我要報警。 ngóh yiu bou gíng

Health

Essential

I'm sick [ill].	我病咗。 ngóh behng jó
I need an English-speaking doctor.	我需要講英文嘅醫生。 ngóh sēui yiu góng yīng màhn ge yī sāng
It hurts here.	呢度痛。 nī douh tung
I have a stomachache.	我肚痛。 ngóh tóu tung

Finding a Doctor

Can you recommend a *doctor/dentist*?	你可唔可以介紹一位醫生/牙醫? néih hó m hó yíh gaai siuh yāt wái *yīsāng/ngàh yī*

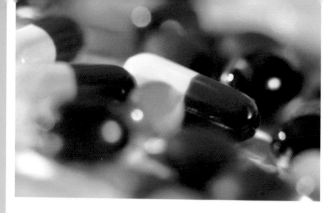

Can the doctor come here?	醫生可唔可以嚟呢度? yī sāng hó m hó yíh làih nī douh
I need an English-speaking doctor.	我需要講英文嘅醫生。ngóh sēui yiu góng yīng màhn ge yī sāng
What are the office hours?	辦公時間係幾時? baahn gūng sìh gaan haih géi sìh
I'd like an appointment for…	我想要同…預約。ngóh séung yiu tùhng…yuh yeuk
– today	– 今日 gām yaht
– tomorrow	– 聽日 tīng yaht
– as soon as possible	– 儘快 jeuhn faai
It's urgent.	好急。hóu gāp

Symptoms

I'm…	我… ngóh…
– bleeding	– 流緊血 làuh gán hyut
– constipated	– 便秘 bihn bei
– dizzy	– 頭暈 tàuh wàhn

– nauseous	– 想嘔 séung ngáu
– vomiting	– 嘔 ngáu
It hurts here.	呢度痛。nī douh tung
I have…	我… ngóh…
– an allergic reaction	– 有過敏反應 yáuh gwo máhn fáan ying
– chest pain	– 心口痛 sām háu tung
– cramps	– 有抽筋 yáuh chāu gān
– a cut	– 有傷口 yáuh sēung háu
– diarrhea	– 肚屙 tóuh ngō
– discharge	– 排瀉物 pàaih sit maht
– an earache	– 耳仔痛 yíh jái tung
– a fever	– 發燒 faat sīu
– pain	– 痛 tung
– a rash	– 出疹 chēut chán
– a sprain	– 扭傷 náu sēung
– some swelling	– 有腫 yáuh júng
– a sore throat	– 喉嚨痛 hàuh lùhng tung
– a stomachache	– 肚痛 tóuh tung
– sunstroke	– 中暑 jung syú
I've been sick [ill] for…days.	我病咗已經…日喇。ngóh behng jó yíh gīng…yaht la

▶ For numbers, see page 157.

Health Conditions

| I'm anemic. | 我有貧血。ngóh yáuh pàhn hyut |
| I'm allergic to antibiotics. | 我對抗生素過敏。ngóh deui kong sāng sou gwo máhn |

▶ For food items, see page 82.

I have…	我有… ngóh yáuh…
– arthritis	– 關節炎 gwāan jit yìhm
– asthma	– 哮喘 hāau chyún
– a heart condition	– 心臟病 sām johng behng
– diabetes	– 糖尿病 tòhng niuh behng
– *high/low* blood pressure	– 高/低血壓 *gōu/dāi* hyut ngaat
I'm on…	我喺食… ngóh haih sihk…

You May Hear…

點樣? dím yéung	What's wrong?
邊度痛? bīn douh tung	Where does it hurt?
呢度痛唔痛? nī douh tung m tung	Does it hurt here?
你食緊藥? néih sihk gán yeuhk	Are you on medication?
你對乜野過敏? néih deui māt yéh gwo máhn	Are you allergic to anything?
打開口。dá hōi háu	Open your mouth.
深呼吸。sām fū kāp	Breathe deeply.
唔該咳一下。m gōi kāt yāt háh	Cough, please.
去睇專科。heui tái jyūn fō	See a specialist.
去醫院。heui yī yún	Go to the hospital.
你… néih…	It's…
– 骨折 gwāt jit	– broken
– 會傳染 wúih chyùhn yíhm	– contagious
– 有感染 yáuh gám yíhm	– infected
– 扭傷 náuh sēung	– sprained
– 唔緊要 m gán yiu	– nothing serious

Treatment

Do I need medicine?	我需唔需要食藥? ngóh sēui m sēui yiu sihk yeuhk
Can you prescribe a generic drug [unbranded medication]?	你可唔可以開常用藥? néih hó m hó yíh hōi sèuhng yuhng yeuhk
Where can I get it?	我喺邊度可以買到? ngóh hái bīn douh hó yíh máaih dóu

▶ For dosage instructions, see page 151.

Hospital

Notify my family, please.	唔該通知我家人。 m gōi tūng jī ngóh gā yàhn
I'm in pain.	我好痛。 ngóh hóu tung
I need a *doctor/nurse*.	我需要醫生/護士。 ngóh sēui yiu *yī sāng/ wuh sih*
When are visiting hours?	探病時間係幾時? taam behng sìh gaan haih géi sìh
I'm visiting…	我嚟探… ngóh làih taam…

Dentist

I have…	我… ngóh…
– a broken tooth	– 有一隻爛牙 yáuh yāt jek laahn ngàh
– lost a filling	– 嘅補牙甩咗 ge bóu ngàh lāt jó
– a toothache	– 牙痛 ngàh tung
Can you fix this denture?	你可唔可以修補呢隻假牙? néih hó m hó yíh sāu bóu nī jek gá ngàh

Gynecologist

I have *cramps/ a vaginal infection*.	我有經期腹痛/陰道感染。 ngóh yáuh *gīng kèih fūk tung/yām douh gám yíhm*

I missed my period.	我月經未嚟。 ngóh yuht gīng meih làih
I'm on the Pill.	我食緊避孕藥。 ngóh sihk gán beih yahn yeuhk
I'm (…months) pregnant.	我有咗（…月）。 ngóh yáuh jó (…yuht)
I'm not pregnant.	我有懷孕。 ngóh móuh wàaih yahn
My last period was…	我上次月經係… ngóh seuhng chi yuht gīng haih…

Optician

I lost…	我唔見咗… ngóh m gin jó…
– a contact lens	– 隱形眼鏡 yán yìhng ngáahn géng
– my glasses	– 我嘅眼鏡 ngóh ge geng pín
– a lens	– 一塊鏡片 yāt faai geng pín

Payment and Insurance

How much?	幾多錢? géi dō chín
Can I pay by credit card?	我可唔可以用信用卡畀錢? ngóh hó m hó yíh yuhng seun yuhng kāat béi chín
I have insurance.	我有保險。 ngóh yáuh bóu hím
I need a receipt for my insurance.	我需要保險收據。 ngóh sēui yiu bóu hím sāu geui

Pharmacy [Chemist]

Essential

| Where's the pharmacy [chemist]? | 藥房喺邊度? yeuhk fòhng hái bīn douh |
| What time does it *open/close*? | 幾時開門/閂門? géi sìh *hōi mùhn/sāan mùhn* |

150

What would you recommend for…?	你對…有乜野推薦呢? néih deui…yáuh māt yéh tēui jin nē
How much do I take?	我要食幾多呢? ngóh yiu sihk géi dō nē
Can you fill [make up] this prescription?	你可唔可以提供呢種處方藥? néih hó m hó yíh tàih gūng nī júng chyúh fōng yeuhk
I'm allergic to…	我對…敏感。 ngóh deui…máhn gám

---

i

You will likely find some 24-hour pharmacies in larger cities. Standard pharmacy hours are 9 a.m. to 9 p.m. In the event of an emergency, visit the nearest hospital emergency center.

China is well known for its traditional pharmacies, 中藥 **jūng yeuhk**, which provide many natural remedies: dried and preserved plants, seeds, animal parts and minerals. You may also find acupuncture needles and other holistic healing tools at these locations.

Dosage Instructions

How much do I take?	我食幾多呢? ngóh sihk géi dō nē
How often?	幾耐食一次? géi noih sihk yāt chi
Is it safe for children?	對細蚊仔安唔安全? deui sai mān jái ngōn m ngōn chyùhn
I'm taking…	我食緊… ngóh sihk gán…
Are there side effects?	有冇副作用? yáuh móuh fu jok yuhng

You May See…

| 一日一次/三次 yāt yaht *yāt chi/sāam chi* | *once/three times* a day |
| 藥丸 yeuhk yún | tablet |

滴劑 dihk jāi	drop
用茶羹食 yuhng chàh ngāng sihk	teaspoon
飯後/飯前/食飯時服用 faahn hauh/ faahn chìhn/sihk faahn sìh fuhk yuhng	*after/before/with meals*
空肚服用 hūng tóuh fuhk yuhng	on an empty stomach
整個吞下 jíng go tān hah	swallow whole
使人有睡意 sí yàhn yáuh seuih yi	may cause drowsiness
只能外用 jí nàhng noih yuhng	for external use only

Health Problems

I need something for…	我需要醫⋯嘅藥。 ngóh sēui yiu yī…ge yeuhk
– a cold	– 感冒 gám mouh
– a cough	– 咳 kāt
– diarrhea	– 肚屙 tóu ngō
– a hangover	– 宿醉 sūk jeui
– insect bites	– 蟲咬 chùhng ngáauh
– motion [travel] sickness	– 暈浪 wàhn lohng
– a sore throat	– 喉嚨痛 hàuh lùhng tung
– sunburn	– 曬傷 saai sēung
– an upset stomach	– 腸胃不適 chuhng waih bāt sīk

Basic Needs

I'd like…	我要⋯ ngóh yiu…
– aftershave	– 鬚後水 sōu hauh séui
– aspirin	– 阿斯匹靈 a sih pāt nìhng
– bandages	– 繃帶 bāng dáai

– a comb	– 一把梳 yat bá sō
– condoms	– 避孕套 beih yahn tou
– contact lens solution	– 隱形眼鏡藥水 yán yìhng ngáhn geng yeuhk séui
– deodorant	– 止汗劑 jí hohn jāi
– a hairbrush	– 一把梳 yāt bá sō
– hairspray	– 噴髮劑 pan faat jāi
– insect repellent	– 殺蟲劑 saat chùhng jāi
– lotion	– 乳液 yúh yihk
– a nail file	– 指甲銼 jí gaap cho
– a (disposable) razor	– (即棄) 剃鬚刀 (jīk hei) tai sōu dōu
– razor blades	– 刀片 dōu pín
– rubbing alcohol [surgical spirit]	– 外用酒精 ngoih yuhng jáu jīng
– sanitary napkins [pads]	– 衛生巾 waih sāng gān
– shampoo/ conditioner	– 洗頭水/護髮素 sái tàuh séui/wuhn faat sou
– soap	– 番鹼 fāan gáan
– sunscreen	– 防曬霜 fòhng saai sēung
– tampons	– 棉條 mìhn tíu
– tissues	– 紙巾 jí gān
– toilet paper	– 廁紙 chi jí
– a toothbrush	– 牙刷 ngàh chaat
– toothpaste	– 牙膏 ngàh gōu

▶For basic needs for kids, see page 138.

Reference

Grammar

Verbs

Chinese verbs are not conjugated. There is one basic verb form that is used for every person and tense. Expressing tense is usually done through adverbs of time—yesterday, tomorrow, etc.—e.g.,

I walk to school every day. (habitual action)
我每日行路去學校。
ngóh múih yaht hàahng louh heui hohk haauh

We want to go to school on foot. (talking about a plan)
我想行路去學校。
ngóh séung hàahng louh heui hohk haauh

I walked to school. (talking about a past event)
我係行去學校嘅。
ngóh haih hàahng heui hohk haauh ge

Tense can also be expressed by using the particle 過 (gwo) or 咗 (jó), e.g.,

I have eaten.
我食咗飯喇。
ngóh sihk jó faahn la

Nouns

There are no plural forms for Chinese nouns, with few exceptions. Whether the noun is singular or plural is determined from the context or by a number modifying the noun.

My bag is missing.
我嘅袋唔見咗。
ngóh ge dói m gin jó

My bags are missing.
我啲袋唔見咗。
ngóh dī dói m gin jó

Pronouns

Personal pronouns in Chinese are:

I	我	ngóh
you	你	néih
he	佢	kéuih
she	佢	kéuih
it	佢	kéuih
we	我哋	ngóh deih
you (pl.)	你哋	néih deih
they	佢哋	kéuih deih

Personal pronouns do not require different verb forms, e.g.,

I am	我係	ngóh haih
He is	佢係	kéuih haih
They are	佢哋係	kéuih deih haih

Add 嘅 (ge) after the pronoun to make it possessive, e.g.,

my	我嘅	ngóh ge (Literally: I + ge)

Word Order

Word order in Chinese is usually as in English: subject, verb, object. This varies, though, depending on the emphasis of the sentence.

I would like a cup of tea.
我想要杯茶。
ngóh séung yiu būi chàh

Yes/No questions are formed by using a verb-not-verb structure, e.g.,

Is this the ticket office? (Literally: Here to be not to be ticket office?)
呢度係唔係售票處?
nī douh haih m haih sau piu chyu

Other questions are formed by inserting specific question words—who, what, where, when, how many, etc.—in the sentence where the information asked for would come, e.g.,

<u>Where</u> is the ticket office?
售票處喺邊度?
sauh piu chyu hái bīn douh

The Chinese is literally, "Ticket office is <u>where</u>?" "Where" follows the verb because the answer would also follow the verb, "The ticket office is <u>here</u>."

Negation and Affirmation

唔 (m) or 冇 (móuh) is added before the verb to indicate negation. While 唔 usually preceeds the verb to be, 冇 is used in front of 有 (yáuh) and to negate action already completed. For example:

I am not on vacation.
我唔係度緊假。
ngóh m haih douh gán ga

I have not bought the ticket.
我仲未買飛。
ngóh juhng meih máaih fēi

Repeat the verb that was used in the question for affirmations or add 唔 (m) before the verb for negations.

Would you like tea?
你想唔想飲茶?
néih séung m séung yám chàh

Yes, I would.
想。
séung

No, thank you.
唔想。
m séung

Imperatives

Usually, 啦 (lā) or 呀 (a) is added at the end of a statement to express a command politely, for example:

Buy the ticket!   買飛票啦! máaih fēi lā

Adjectives

Adjectives with two or more syllables in Chinese usually have the character 嘅 (ge) at the end and precede the noun they modify, for example:

| a good meal | 好食嘅野 hóu sihk ge yéh |

Adverbs

Adverbs in Chinese are usually followed by 咁 (gám) and precede the verbs they modify, for example:

| work carefully | 認真咁工作 yihng jān gám gūng jok |

Numbers ─────────────────────────

Essential	
0	零 lìhng
1	一 yāt
2	二 yih
3	三 sāam
4	四 sei
5	五 ngh
6	六 luhk
7	七 chāt
8	八 baat
9	九 gáu
10	十 sahp
11	十一 sahp yāt
12	十二 sahp yih
13	十三 sahp sāam
14	十四 sahp sei

15	十五 sahp ngh
16	十六 sahp luhk
17	十七 sahp chāt
18	十八 sahp baat
19	十九 sahp gáu
20	二十 yih sahp
21	二十一 yih sahp yāt
22	二十二 yih sahp yiih
30	三十 sāam sahp
31	三十一 sāam sahp yāt
40	四十 sei sahp
50	五十 ngh sahp
60	六十 luhk sahp
70	七十 chāt sahp
80	八十 baat sahp
90	九十 gáu sahp
100	一百 yāt baak
101	一百零一 yāt baak lìhng yāt
200	二百 yih baak
500	五百 ngh baak
1,000	一千 yāt chīn
10,000	一萬 yāt maahn
1,000,000	一百萬 yāt baak maahn

In Chinese, there are general numbers, listed above, used for talking about sums of money, phone numbers, etc. There is also a system for combining a number with an object-specific counter. This system groups objects into types according to shape and size; there are specific ways to count flat objects, machines, animals, people, etc. When you're unsure of the correct counter, you can try using the general numbers above or the all-purpose counters that follow.

All-purpose Counters

1	一個	yāt go
2	兩個	léuhng go
3	三個	sāam go
4	四個	sei go
5	五個	ngh go
6	六個	sahp go
7	七個	chāt go
8	八個	baat go
9	九個	gáu go
10	十個	sahp go

Note that the counter usually precedes the word it qualifies, for example:

I'd like an apple.
我想要一個蘋果。
ngóh séung yiu yāt go pìhng gwó

I'd like two apples.
我想要兩個蘋果。
ngóh séung yiu léuhng go pìhng gwó

Other Counters

	thin, flat objects	small objects (of any shape)	packages (of any size)
1	一張 yāt jēung	一塊 yāt faai	一包 yāt bāau
2	兩張 léuhng jēung	兩塊 léuhng faai	兩包 léuhng bāau
3	三張 sāam jēung	三塊 sāam faai	三包 sāam bāau
4	四張 sei jēung	四塊 sei faai	四包 sei bāau
5	五張 ngh jēung	五塊 ngh faai	五包 ngh bāau

Ordinal Numbers

first	第一 daih yāt
second	第二 daih yih
third	第三 daih sāam
fourth	第四 daih sei
fifth	第五 daih ngh

Measurements of Action

once	一次 yāt chi
twice	兩次 léuhng chi
three times	三次 sāam chi

Time

What time is it?	幾點? géi dím
It's noon [midday].	而家係中午。 yìh gā haih jūng ngh
At midnight.	喺午夜。 hái ngh yeh
From one o'clock to two o'clock.	由一點到兩點。 yàuh yāt dím dou léuhng dím

Five after [past] three.	三點零五分。 sāam dím lìhng ngh fān
5:30 *a.m./p.m.*	上晝/下晝五點半 *seuhng jau/hah jau* ngh dím bun

Days

Monday	星期一 sīng kèih yāt
Tuesday	星期二 sīng kèih yih
Wednesday	星期三 sīng kèih sāam
Thursday	星期四 sīng kèih sei
Friday	星期五 sīng kèih ngh
Saturday	星期六 sīng kèih luhk
Sunday	星期日 sīng kèih yaht

Dates

yesterday	琴日	kàhm yaht
today	今日	gām yaht
tomorrow	聽日	tīng yaht
day	日	yaht
week	星期	sīng kèih
month	月	yuht
year	年	nìhn

> In China, dates are written in the following order: year 年
> (**nihn**), month 月 (**yuht**) and date 日 (**yaht**). For example,
> October 12, 2008 in Chinese would be **2008**年**10**月**12**日.
> Note that while months can be represented as following,
> Arabic numbers are also used.

Months

January	一月	yāt yuht
February	二月	yih yuht
March	三月	sāam yuht
April	四月	sei yuht
May	五月	ngh yuht
June	六月	luhk yuht
July	七月	chāt yuht
August	八月	baat yuht
September	九月	gáu yuht
October	十月	sahp yuht
November	十一月	sahp yāt yuht
December	十二月	sahp yih yuht

Seasons

spring	春天 chēun tīn
summer	夏天 hah tīn
fall [autumn]	秋天 chāu tīn
winter	冬天 dūng tīn

Holidays

1st Day of the 1st Lunar Month: Spring Festival (Chinese New Year)

May 1: International Labor Day

May 5 (Lunar Calendar): Dragon Boat Festival

October 1: National Day

October 15 (Lunar Calendar): Mid-Autumn Festival (Moon-cake Day)

> **i** Traditional holidays, such as Chinese New Year, or Spring Festival, follow the lunar calendar and, so, dates vary annually. Chinese New Year is an important holiday in China, celebrated with gifts, decorations, traditional food and fireworks. It ends on the fifteenth day of the lunar new year with the Lantern Festival, which includes festivities such as a lantern parade and lion dance.

Conversion Tables

When you know	Multiply by	To find
ounces	28.3	grams
pounds	0.45	kilograms
inches	2.54	centimeters
feet	0.3	meters
miles	1.61	kilometers
square inches	6.45	sq. centimeters

square feet	0.09	sq. meters
square miles	2.59	sq. kilometers
pints (US/Brit)	0.47/0.56	liters
gallons (US/Brit)	3.8/4.5	Centigrade
Centigrade	9/5, then +32	Fahrenheit

Mileage

1 km – 0.62 mi	20 km – 12.4 mi
5 km – 3.1 mi	50 km – 31 mi
10 km – 6.2 mi	100 km – 61 mi

Measurement

1 gram	克 hāk	= 0.035 oz.
1 kilogram (kg)	公斤 gūnggān	= 2.2 lb
1 liter (l)	公升 gūng sīng	= 1.06 U.S/0.88 Brit. quarts
1 centimeter (cm)	釐米 lèih mái	= 0.4 inch
1 meter (m)	米 máih	= 3.28 feet
1 kilometer (km)	公里 gūng léih	= 0.62 mile

Temperature

-40° C – -40° F	-1° C – 30° F	20° C – 68° F
-30° C – -22° F	0° C – 32° F	25° C – 77° F
-20° C – -4° F	5° C – 41° F	30° C – 86° F
-10° C – 14° F	10° C – 50° F	35° C – 95° F
-5° C – 23° F	15° C – 59° F	

Oven Temperature

100° C – 212° F   177° C – 350° F

Useful Websites

For airport safety information
www.tsa.gov (U.S.)
www.caa.co.uk (U.K.)

For general tourism information about China
www.chinahighlights.com
www.chinatravel.com
www.chinatour.com

For Chinese tourist information offices
www.cnto.org
www.cytstours.com
www.citsusa.com
www.chinatravelservice.com

For the Hong Kong Tourism Board website
www.discoverhongkong.com

For hostel reservations and information
www.hihostels.com

For Berlitz Publishing products
www.berlitzpublishing.com

English–Chinese Dictionary

A

accept *v* 接受 jip sauh

access 進入 jeun yahp

accident 意外 yi ngoih

accommodation 住宿 jyuh sūk

account 帳戶 jeung wuh

acupuncture 針灸 jām gau

adapter 變壓器 bin ngaat hei

address 地址 deih jí

admission 入場 yahp chèuhng

after 以後 yíh hauh

aftershave 鬚後水 sōu hauh séui

age 年齡 nìhn nìhng

agency 代辦處 doih baahn chyu

air conditioning 冷氣 láahng hei

air pump 氣泵 hei bām

airline 航空公司 hòhng hūng gūng sī

airmail 航空信 hòhng hūng seun

airplane 飛機 fēi gēi

airport 飛機場 fēi gēi chèuhng

aisle seat 路口位 louh háu wái

allergic 敏感 máhn gám

allergic reaction 過敏反應 gwo máhn fáan ying

allow *v* 准許 jéun héui

alone 單獨 dāan duhk

alter *v* (clothing) 改 gói

alternate route 更改路線 gāng gói louh sin

aluminum foil 錫紙 sehk jí

amazing 令人驚奇嘅 lihng yàhn gīng kèih ge

ambulance 救護車 gau sēung chē

American 美國人 méih gwok yàhn

amusement park 遊樂園 yàuh lohk yùhn

anemic 貧血 pàhn hyut

anesthesia 麻醉 màh jeui

animal 動物 duhng maht

ankle 腳眼 geuk ngáahn

antibiotic 抗生素 kong sāng sou

antiques store 古董店 gú dúng dim

adj	adjective	BE	British English	n	noun
v	verb				

antiseptic cream 消毒藥膏 sīu duhk yeuk gōu

anything 任何野 yahm hòh yéh

apartment 公寓 gūng yuh

appendix (body part) 盲腸 màahng chéung

appetizer 開胃菜 hōi waih choi

appointment 約 yeuk

area code 區號 kēui houh

arm 手臂 sáu bei

aromatherapy 香薰療法 hēung fān lìuh faat

around (the corner) 轉角處 jyun gok chyu

arrivals (airport) 抵達 dái daaht

arrive v 到達 dou daaht

artery 動脈 duhng mahk

arthritis 關節炎 gwāan jit yìhm

Asian (restaurant) 亞洲 nga jāu

aspirin 阿斯匹零 a sī pāt lìhng

asthmatic 氣喘 hei chyún

ATM 自動提款機 jih duhng tàih fún gēi

ATM card 自動提款卡 jih duhng tàih fún kāat

attack (on person) 攻擊 gūng gīk

attend v 出席 chēut jihk

attraction (place) 遊覽勝地 yàuh láahm sing deih

attractive 有吸引力嘅 yáuh kāp yáhn lihk ge

Australia 澳洲 ou jāu

B

baby BB bìh bī

baby bottle 奶樽 náaih jēung

baby wipe 嬰兒紙巾 yīng yìh jí gān

babysitter 保姆 bóu móuh

back (body part) 背脊 bui jek

backache 背痛 bui tung

backpack 背囊 bui nòhng

bag 袋 dói

baggage [BE] 行李 hàhng léih

baggage claim 行李認領 hàhng léih yihng léhng

baggage ticket 行李票 hàhng léih piu

bakery 麵包鋪 mihn bāau póu

ballet 芭蕾 bā lèuih

bandage 繃帶 bāng dáai

bank 銀行 ngàhn hòhng

bar (place) 酒吧 jáu bā

barbecue 烤肉 hāau yuhk

barber 理髮師 léih faat sī

baseball 棒球 páahng kàuh

basket (grocery store) 購物籃 kau maht láam

basketball 籃球 làahm kàuh

bathroom 沖涼房 chūng lèuhng fóng

battery 電芯 dihn sām

battleground 戰場 jin chèuhng

be v 會係 wúih haih

beach 海灘 hói tāan

beautiful 靚 leng

bed 床 chòhng

bed and breakfast 有早餐嘅酒店 yáuh jóu chāan ge jáu dim

begin v 開始 hōi chí

before 以前 yíh chìhn

beginner (skill level) 初學者 chō hohk jé

behind (direction) 後面 hauh mihn

beige 米黃色 máih wòhng sīk

belt 皮帶 pèih dáai

berth 鋪位 pou wái

best 最好 jeui hóu

better 好啲 hóu dī

bicycle 單車 dāan chē

big 大 daaih

bike route 單車路線 dāan chē louh sin

bikini 比基尼裝 béi gīn nèih jōng

bill v (charge) 開單 hōi dāan; n (money) 紙幣 jí baih; n (of sale) 單 dāan

bird 雀仔 jeuk jái

birthday 生日 sāang yaht

black 黑色 hāk sīk

bladder 膀胱 pòhng gwōng

bland 無味 mòuh meih

blanket 毯 jīn

bleed v 流血 làuh hyut

blood 血液 hyut yihk

blood pressure 血壓 hyut ngaat

blouse 女裝恤衫 néuih jōng sēut sāam

blue 藍色 làahm sīk

board v 登機 dāng gēi

boarding pass 登機証 dāng gēi jing

boat 船 syùhn

bone 骨頭 gwāt tàuh

book 書 syū

bookstore 書店 syū dim

boots 靴 hēu

boring 無聊嘅 mòuh lìuh ge

botanical garden 植物園 jihk maht yùhn

bother v 打攪 dá gáau

bottle 樽 jēun

bottle opener 開瓶器 hōi pìhng hei

bowl 碗 wún

box 箱 sēung

boxing match 拳擊比賽 kyùhn gīk béi choi

boy 男仔 nàahm jái

boyfriend 男朋友 nàahm pàhng yáuh

bra 胸圍 hūng wàih

bracelet 手扼 sáu ngáak

break v (tooth) 爛 laahn

break-in (burglary) 闖入 chóng yahp

breakdown 故障 gu jeung

breakfast 早餐 jóu chāan

breast 乳房 yúh fòhng

breastfeed 餵母乳 wai móuh yúh

breathe v 呼吸 fū kāp

bridge 橋樑 kìuh lèuhng

briefs (clothing) 緊身褲 gán sān fu

bring v 帶嚟 daai làih

British 英國人 yīng gwok yàhn

broken 爛咗 laahn jó

brooch 心口針 sām háu jām

broom 帚把 sou bá

brother 兄弟 hīng daih

brown 咖啡色 ga fē sīk

bug 蟲 chùhng

building 大廈 daaih hah

burn v 燒 sīu

bus 巴士 bā sí

bus station 巴士站 bā sí jaahm

bus stop 巴士站 bā sí jaahm

bus ticket 巴士車票 bā sí chē piu

bus tour 巴士遊覽 bā sí yàuh láahm

business 商務 sēung mouh

business card 咭片 kāat pín

business center 商業中心 sēung yihp jūng sām

business class 商務艙 sēung mouh chōng

business hours 營業時間 yìhng yihp sìh gaan

buttocks 屁股 pei gú

buy v 買 máaih

bye 再見 joi gin

C

cabin 客艙 haak chōng

café 咖啡館 ga fē gún

call v 打電話 dá dihn wá; n 電話 dihn wá

calligraphy supplies 書法用品 syū faat yuhng bán

calories 卡路里 kā louh léih

camera 相機 séung gēi

camera case 相機套 séung gēi tou

camera store 攝影器材商店 sip yíng hei chòih sēung dim

camp v 露營 louh yìhng

camping stove 露營爐 louh yìhng lòuh

campsite 營地 yìhng deih

can opener 開罐器 hōi gun hei

Canada 加拿大 ga nàh daaih

cancel v 取消 chéui sīu

canyon 峽谷 haap gūk

car 汽車 hei chē

car hire [BE] 出租汽車 chēut jōu hei chē

car park [BE] 停車場 tìhng chē chèuhng

car rental 出租汽車 chēut jōu hei chē

car seat 汽車座位 hei chē joh wái

carafe 碴 jā

card 卡 kāat

carry-on 手提行李 sáu tàih hàhng léih

cart (grocery store) 手推車 sáu tēui chē

cart (luggage) 行李車 hàhng léih chē

case (amount) 件 gihn

cash v 換現金 wuhn yihn gām; n 現金 yihn gām

cash advance 預支現金 yuh jī yìhn gām

cashier 出納員 chēut naahp yùhn

casino 賭場 dóu chèuhng

castle 城堡 sìhng bóu

cathedral 大教堂 daaih gaau tòhng

cave 山洞 sāan duhng

CD CD sī dī

cell phone 手機 sáu gēi

Celsius 攝氏 sip sih

centimeter 釐米 lèih máih

ceramic spoon 湯羹 tōng gāng

certificate 證明 jing mìhng

chair 凳 dang

change v (buses) 換車 wuhn chē; v (money) 換錢 wuhn chín; v (baby) 換尿片 wuhn niuh pín; n (money) 散紙 sáan jí

charcoal 木炭 muhk taan

charge v (credit card) 用信用卡畀錢 yuhng seun yuhng kāa béi chín; n (cost) 收費 sāu fai

cheap 平 pèhng

check v (something) 檢查 gím chàh; v (luggage) 托運 tok wahn; n (payment) 支票 jī piu

check-in (airport) 辦理登機手續 baahn léih dāng gēi sáu juhk

checking account 支票戶口 jī piu wuh háu

check-out (hotel) 退房 teui fóng

chemist [BE] 藥劑師 yeuhk jāi sī

cheque [BE] 支票 jī piu

chest (body part) 心口 sām háu

chest pain 心口痛 sām háu tung

chewing gum 香口膠 hēung háu gāau

child 細蚊仔 sai mān jái

child's seat BB凳 bìh bī dang

children's menu 兒童菜單 yìh tùhng choi dāan

children's portion 兒童飯量 yìh tùhng faahn leuhng

china 瓷器 chìh hei

China 中國 jūng gwok

Chinese 中文 jūng màhn

Chinese painting 中國畫 jūng gwok wá

chopsticks 筷子 faai jí

church 教堂 gaau tóng

cigar 雪茄 syut kā

cigarette 煙 yīn

class 艙 chōng

clay pot 砂鍋 sā wō

cloisonné 景泰藍 gíng taai làahm

first class 頭等艙 tàuh dáng chōng

classical music 古典音樂 gú dín yām ngohk

clean v 洗 sái; adj 乾淨 gōn jehng

cleaning product 清潔產品 chīng git cháan bán

clear v (on an ATM) 清除 chīng chèuih

cliff 懸崖 yùhn ngàaih

cling film [BE] 保鮮紙 bóu sīn jí

close v (a shop) 關門 gwāan mùhn; adj 近 kahn

closed 關閉 gwāan bai

clothing 衣物 yī maht

clothing store 時裝店 sìh jōng dim

club 俱樂部 kēui lohk bouh

coat 外套 ngoih tou

coffee shop 咖啡店 ga fē dim

coin 硬幣 ngaahng beih

cold (sickness) 感冒 gám mouh;
(temperature) 冷 láahng

colleague 同事 tùhng sih

cologne 古龍水 gú lùhng séui

color 顏色 ngàahn sīk

comb 梳 sō

come v 嚟 làih

complaint 投訴 tàuh sou

computer 電腦 dihn nóuh

concert 音樂會 yām ngohk wúi

concert hall 音樂廳 yām ngohk
tēng

condition (medical) 症狀 jing
johng

conditioner 護髮素 wuh faat
sou

condom 避孕套 beih yan tou

conference 會議 wuih yíh

confirm v 證實 jing saht

congestion 充血 chūng hyut

connect v (internet) 連接 lìhn
jip

connection (internet) 連接
lìhn jip; (flight) 轉機 jyun gēi

constipated 便秘 bin bei

consulate 領事館 líhng sih gún

consultant 顧問 gu mahn

contact v 聯繫 lyùhn haih

contact lens 隱形眼鏡 yán
yìhng ngáahn géng

contact lens solution 隱形眼
鏡液 yán yìhng ngáahn géng
yihk

contagious 傳染嘅 chyùhn
yíhm ge

convention hall 會議廳 wuih
yíh tēng

cook v 烹調 pāang tìuh

cooking gas 烹調煤氣 pāang
tìuh mùih hei

cool (temperature) 涼 lèuhng

copper 銅 tùhng

corkscrew 開酒器 hōi jáu hei

cost v 用 yuhng

cot 床仔 chòhng jái

cotton 棉花 mìhn fā

cough n/v 咳 kāt

country code 國家代號 gwok
gā doih houh

cover charge 附加費 fuh gā fai

crash v (car) 撞 johng

cream (ointment) 藥膏 yeuhk
gōu

credit card 信用卡 seun yuhng
kāat

crib 搖籃 yìuh láam

crystal 水晶 séui jīng

cup 杯 būi

currency 貨幣 fo baih

currency exchange 貨幣兌換 fo baih deui wuhn

currency exchange office 貨幣兌換局 fo baih deui wuhn gúk

current account [BE] 支票戶口 jī piu wuh háu

customs 海關 hói gwāan

cut v (hair) 剪 jín; n (injury) 傷口 sēung háu

cute 得意 dāk yi

cycling 踩單車 cháai dāan chē

D

damage v 損傷 syún sēung

damaged 壞咗 waaih jó

dance v 跳舞 tiu móuh

dance club 舞蹈俱樂部 móuh douh kēui lohk bouh

dangerous 危險 ngàih hím

dark 黑暗 hāk ngam

date (calendar) 日期 yaht kèih

day 日 yaht

deaf 聾 lùhng

debit card 借記卡 je gei kāat

declare v 申報 sān bou

decline v (credit card) 拒絕 kéuih jyuht

degrees (temperature) 度 douh

delay v 遲啲 chìh dī

delete v 刪除 sāan chèuih

delicatessen 熟食 suhk sihk

delicious 好食 hóu sihk

denim 牛仔布 ngàuh jái bou

dentist 牙醫 ngàh yī

denture 假牙 gá ngàh

deodorant 止汗劑 jí hon jāi

department store 百貨公司 baak fo gūng sī

departure 離開 lèih hōi

deposit v 存錢 chyùhn chín; n (bank) 儲蓄 chyúh chūk

desert 沙漠 sā mohk

diabetic 糖尿病 tòhng niuh behng

dial v 撥號 buht houh

diamond 鑽石 jyun sehk

diaper 尿片 niuh pín

diarrhea 肚屙 tóu ngō

diesel 柴油 chàih yàuh

difficult 困難 kwan nàahn

digital 數碼 sou máh

digital camera 數碼相機 sou máh séung gēi

digital photo 數碼相片 sou máh seung pín

digital print 數碼印刷品 sou máh yan chaat bán

dining room 飯廳 faahn tēng

dinner 晚餐 máahn chāan

direction 方向 fōng heung

dirty 污糟 wū jōng

disabled 殘疾 chàahn jaht

disabled accessible [BE] 殘疾人通道 chàahn jaht yàhn tūng douh

disconnect (computer) 斷開 tyúhn hōi

discount 折 jit

dish (kitchen) 碟 dihp

dishwasher 洗碗機 sái wún gēi

dishwashing liquid 洗潔精 sái git jīng

display 顯示 hín sih

display case 陳列櫃 chàhn liht gwaih

disposable 即棄 jīk hei

disposable razor 即棄剃鬚刀 jīk hei tai sōu dōu

dive v 潛水 chìhm séui

diving equipment 潛水用具 chìhm séui yuhng geuih

divorce v 離婚 lèih fān

dizzy 頭暈眼花 tàuh wàhn ngáahn fā

doctor 醫生 yī sāng

doll 公仔 gūng jái

dollar (H.K.) 港元 góng yùhn; **(U.S.)** 美元 méih yùhn

domestic 國内 gwok noih

domestic flight 國内航班 gwok noih hòhng bāan

dormitory 宿舍 sūk se

double bed 雙人床 sēung yàhn chòhng

downtown 市中心 síh jūng sām

dozen 一打 yāt dā

dress (piece of clothing) 禮服 láih fuhk

dress code 服裝要求 fuhk jōng yīu kàuh

drink v 飲 yám; n 飲料 yám liuh

drink menu 飲料單 yám liuh dāan

drive v 開車 hōi chē

driver's license number 駕駛執照號碼 ga sái jāp jiu houh máh

drop (medicine) 滴 dihk

drowsiness 睡意 seuih yi

dry cleaner 乾洗店 gōn sái dim

during 期間 kèih gāan

duty (tax) 關稅 gwāan seui

duty-free 免稅 mín seui

DVD DVD dī wī dī

E

ear 耳仔 yíh jái

earache 耳仔痛 yíh jái tung

early 早 jóu

earrings 耳環 yíh wáan

east 東部 dūng bouh

easy 容易 yùhng yih

eat v 食 sihk

economy class 經濟艙 gīng jai chōng

elbow 手掙 sáu jāang

electric outlet 電制 dihn jai

elevator 電梯 dihn tāi

e-mail v 發電郵 faat dihn yàuh; n 電子郵件 dihn jí yàuh gín

e-mail address 電郵地址 dihn yàuh deih jí

emergency 緊急狀態 gán gāp johng taai

emergency exit 緊急出口 gán gāp chēut háu

empty v 倒空 dóu hūng

enamel (jewelry) 琺瑯 faat lòhng

end v 結束 git chūk

English 英文 yīng màhn

engrave v 雕刻 dīu hāk

enjoy v 享用 héung yuhng

enter v 進入 jeun yahp

entertainment 娛樂 yùh lohk

entrance 入口 yahp háu

envelope 信封 seun fūng

epileptic 癲癇 dīn gáan

equipment 設備 chit beih

escalator 自動扶梯 jih duhng fùh tāi

e-ticket 電子票 dihn jí piu

evening 夜晚 yeh máahn

excess 超過 chīu gwo

exchange v (money) 兌換 deui wuhn; v (goods) 交換 gāau wuhn; n (place) 換地方 wuhn deih fōng

exchange rate 兌換率 deui wuhn léut

excursion 遊覽 yàuh láahm

excuse v 原諒 yùhn leuhng

exhausted 用盡 yuhng jeuhn

exit v 出去 chēut heui; n 出口 chēut háu

expensive 昂貴 ngòhng gwai

expert (skill level) 專家 jyūn gā

exposure (film) 曝光 bouh gwōng

express 快 faai

extension (phone) 分機 fān gēi

extra 額外 ngaak ngoih

extra large 加大碼 gā daaih máh

extract v (tooth) 剥 mōk

eye 眼 ngáahn

face 面 mihn

facial 面部 mihn bouh

family 家庭 gā tìhng

fan (appliance) 電風扇 dihn fūng sin

far 遠 yúhn

far-sighted 遠視 yúhn sih

farm 農場 nùhng chèuhng

fast 快速 faai chūk

fast food 快餐 faai chāan

fat free 無脂肪 mòuh jī fōng

father 父親 fuh chān

fax v 發傳真 faat chyùhn jān; n 傳真 chyùhn jān

fax number 傳真號碼 chyùhn jān houh máh

fee 費用 fai yuhng

feed v 餵 wai

ferry 渡輪 douh lèuhn

fever 發燒 faat sīu

field (sports) 運動場 wahn duhng chèuhng

fill out v (form) 填寫 tìhn sé

film (camera) 菲林 fēi lám

fine (fee) 罰款 faht fún

finger 手指 sáu jí

fingernail 指甲 jí gaap

fire 火 fó

fire department 消防隊 sīu fòhng yùhn

fire door 防火門 fòhng fó mùhn

first 第一 daih yāt

first class 頭等艙 tàuh dáng chōng

fit (clothing) 適合 sīk hahp

fitting room 試身室 si sān sāt

fix v (repair) 修理 sāu léih

fixed-price menu 價格固定嘅菜單 ga gaak gu dihng ge choi dāan

flashlight 電筒 dihn túng

flight 航班 hòhng bāan

floor 地板 deih báan

florist 賣花人 maaih fā yàhn

flower 花 fā

folk music 民間音樂 màhn gāan yām ngohk

food 食物 sihk maht

foot 腳 geuk

football game [BE] 足球賽 jūk kàuh choi

for 為咗 waih jó

forecast 預報 yuh bou

forest 森林 sām làhm

fork 叉 chā

form (fill-in) 表格 bíu gaak

formula (baby) 奶粉 náaih fán

fort 要塞 yiu choi

fountain 噴水池 pan séui chìh

free 免費 mín fai

freezer 雪櫃 syut gwaih

fresh 新鮮 sān sīn

friend 朋友 pàhng yáuh

frying pan 煎鍋 jīn wō

full-service 全面服務 chyùhn mihn fuhk móuh

G

game 遊戲 yàuh hei

garage 車房 chē fòhng

garbage 垃圾 laahp saap

garbage bag 垃圾袋 laahp saap dói

gas 汽油 hei yàuh

gas station 加油站 gā yàuh jaahm

gate [airport] 登機門 dāng gēi mùhn

get off (a train/bus/ subway) 落車 lohk chē

gift 禮物 láih maht

gift shop 禮品店 láih bán dim

girl 女仔 néuih jái

girlfriend 女朋友 néuih pàhng yáuh

give v 畀 béi

glass (drinking) 玻璃杯 bō lēi būi

glasses (optical) 眼鏡 ngáahn géng

go v (somewhere) 去 heui

gold 金 gām

golf course 高爾夫球場 gōu yíh fū kàuh chèuhng

golf tournament 高爾夫球比賽 gōu yíh fū kàuh béi choi

good adj/n 好 hóu

good evening 晚安 máahn ngōn

good morning 早晨 jóu sàhn

goodbye 再見 joi gin

goods 貨物 fo maht

gram 克 hāk

grandchild 孫 syūn

grandparent 祖父母 jóu fuh móuh

gray 灰色 fūi sīk

green 綠色 luhk sīk

grocery store 雜貨店 jaahp fo dim

ground floor 一樓 yāt láu

group 小組 síu jóu

guide 指南 jí nàahm

guide book 指南 jí nàahm

guide dog 導盲犬 douh màahng hyún

gym 體操 tái chōu

gynecologist 婦產科醫生 fúh cháan fō yī sāng

H

hair 頭髮 tàuh faat

hair dryer 風筒 fūng túng

hair salon 髮廊 faat lòhng

hairbrush 梳 sō

haircut 飛髮 fēi faat

hairspray 噴髮劑 pan faat jāi

hairstyle 髮型 faat yìhng

hairstylist 髮型師 faat yìhng sī

halal 清真食品 chīng jān sihk bán

half 半 bun

half hour 半小時 bun síu sìh

half-kilo 半公斤 bun gūng gān

hammer 錘 chéui

hand 手 sáu

hand luggage 手提行李 sáu tàih hàhng léih

handbag [BE] 手袋 sáu dói

handicapped 殘疾 chàahn jaht

handicapped-accessible 殘疾人通道 chàahn jaht yàhn tūng douh

hangover 宿醉 sūk jeui

happy 愉快 yuh faai

hat 帽 móu

have v 做 jouh

hay fever 花粉症 fān fán jing

head (body part) 頭 tàuh

headache 頭痛 tàuh tung

headphones 耳筒 yíh túng

health 健康 gihn hōng

health food store 健康食品店 gihn hōng sihk bán dim

hearing impaired 聽力唔好 ting lihk m hóu

heart 心臟 sām johng

heart condition 心臟狀況 sām johng johng fong

heat 加熱 gā yiht

heater 加熱器 gā yiht hei

heating [BE] 暖氣 nyúhng hei

hello 你好 néih hóu

helmet 頭盔 tàuh kwāi

help 幫助 bōng joh

here 呢度 nī douh

hi 你好 néih hóu

high 高 gōu

highchair 高腳椅 gōu geuk yí

highway 高速公路 gōu chūk gūng louh

hill 山仔 sāan jái

hire v [BE] 雇用 gu yuhng

hire car [BE] 租用汽車 jōu yuhng hei chē

hitchhike v 搭車 daap chē

hockey 曲棍球 kūk gwan kàuh

holiday [BE] 假期 ga kèih

horse track 跑馬場 páau máh chèuhng

hospital 醫院 yī yún

hostel 旅舍 léuih se

hot (temperature) 熱 yiht; **(spicy)** 辣 laaht

hot spring 溫泉 wān chyùhn

hotel 酒店 jáu dim

hour 小時 síu sìh

house 屋 ngūk

housekeeping services 客房清潔服務 haak fóng chīng git fuhk móuh

how 點樣 dím yéung

how much 幾多 géi dō

hug v 攬 láam

hungry 餓 ngoh

hurt 痛 tung

husband 老公 lóuh gūng

I

ice 冰 bīng

ice hockey 冰球 bīng kàuh

icy 冰冷 bīng láahng

identification 證件 jing gín

ill [BE] 病 behng

in 喺 hái

include v 包括 bāau kwut

indoor pool 室內泳池 sāt noih wihng chìh

inexpensive 唔貴 m gwai

infected 傳染 chyùhn yíhm

information (phone) 信息 seun sīk

information desk 訊問處 sēun mahn chyu

insect bite 蟲咬 chùhng ngáau

insect repellent 殺蟲劑 saat chùhng jāi

insert v **(on an ATM)** 插入 chaap yahp

insomnia 失眠 sāt mìhn

instant message 即時訊息 jīk sìh seun sīk

insulin 胰島素 yìh dóu sou

insurance 保險 bóu hím

insurance card 保險卡 bóu hím kāat

insurance company 保險公司 bóu hím gūng sī

interesting 有趣 yáuh cheui

international (airport area) 國際 gwok jai

international flight 國際航班 gwok jai hòhng bāan

international student card 國際學生證 gwok jai hohk sāang jing

internet 互聯網 wuh lyùhn móhng

internet cafe 網吧 móhng bā

internet service 互聯網服務 wuh lyùhn móhng fuhk mouh

interpreter 口譯員 háu yihk yùhn

intersection 十字路口 sahp jih louh háu

intestine 腸 chéung

introduce v 介紹 gaai siuh

invoice 發貨單 faat fo dāan

Ireland 愛爾蘭 ngoi yíh làahn

Irish 愛爾蘭人 ngoi yíh làahn yàhn

iron v 熨衫 tong sāam; n 熨斗 tong dáu

jacket 褸 lāu

jade 玉 yúk

jar 磕 jā

jaw 下爬 hah pàh

jazz 爵士樂 jeuk sih ngohk

jazz club 爵士樂俱樂部 jeuk sih ngohk kēui lohk bouh

jeans 牛仔褲 ngáuh jái fu

jeweler 珠寶商 jyū bóu sēung

jewelry 首飾 sáu sīk

join v 加入 gā yahp

joint (body part) 關節 gwāan jit

key 鑰匙 só sìh

key card 鑰匙卡 só sìh kāat

key ring 鑰匙扣 só sìh kau

kiddie pool 兒童泳池 yìh tùhng wihng chìh

kidney (body part) 腎臟 sahn johng

kilogram 公斤 gūng gān

kilometer 公里 gūng léih

kiss v 錫 sek

kitchen 廚房 chyùh fóng

kitchen foil [BE] 廚房錫紙 chyùh fóng sehk jí

knee 膝頭 sāt tàuh

knife 刀 dōu

kosher 猶太食品 yàuh taai sihk bán

L

lace 鞋帶 hàaih dáai

lacquerware 漆器 chāt hei

lactose intolerant 乳糖過敏 yúh tòhng gwo máhn

lake 湖 wùh

large 大 daaih

last 最後 jeui hauh

late (time) 遲咗 chìh jó

launderette [BE] 洗衣店 sái yī dim

laundromat 洗衣店 sái yī dim

laundry 要洗嘅衫 yiu sái ge sāam

laundry facility 洗衣店設施 sái yī dim chit sī

laundry service 洗衣服務 sái yī fuhk mouh

lawyer 律師 leuht sī

leather 皮 péi

leave v 起飛 héi fēi

left (direction) 左邊 jó bīn

leg 腿 téui

lens 鏡片 geng pín

less 比較少 béi gaau síu

lesson 課程 fo chìhng

letter 信件 seun gín

library 圖書館 tòuh syū gún

life jacket 救生衣 gau sāng yī

lifeguard 救生員 gau sāng yùhn

lift v 搭車 daap chē; n [BE] 電梯 dihn tāi

light (overhead) 燈 dāng; **(cigarette)** 點 dím

lightbulb 燈膽 dāng dáam

lighter 打火機 dá fó gēi

like v 鍾意 jūng yi

line (train) 線 sin

linen 麻布 màh bou

lip 嘴唇 jéui sèuhn

liquor store 酒店 jáu dim

liter 公升 gūng sīng

little 少少 síu síu

live v 住 jyuh

liver (body part) 肝臟 gōn johng

loafers 遊蕩者 yàuh dong jé

local 當地 dōng deih

lock n 鎖 só

locker 衣物櫃 yī maht gwaih

log on 登錄 dāng luhk

log off 退出 teui chēut

long 長 chèuhng

long sleeves 長袖 chèuhng jauh

long-sighted [BE] 有遠見 yáuh yúhn gin

look *v* 睇 tái

lose *v* (something) 唔見咗 m gin jó

lost 失去 sāt heui

lost and found 失物認領處 sāt maht yihng líhng chyu

lotion 化妝乳液 fa jōng yúh yihk

love *n/v* (someone) 愛 ngoi

low 低 dāi

luggage 行李 hàhng léih

luggage cart 行李推車 hàhng léih tēui chē

luggage locker 行李暫存箱 hàhng léih jaahm chyùhn sēung

luggage ticket 行李票 hàhng léih piu

lunch 午餐 ngh chāan

lung 肺 fai

M

magazine 雜誌 jaahp ji

magnificent 壯觀 jong gūn

mail *v* 郵寄 yàuh gei; *n* 郵件 yàuh gín

mailbox 郵箱 yàuh sēung

main attraction 主要景點 jyú yiu gíng dím

main course 主菜 jyú choi

make up *v* [BE] (a prescription) 藥方 yeuhk fōng

mall 購物中心 kau maht jūng sām

man 男人 nàahm yán

manager 經理 gīng léih

manicure 修手甲 sāu sáu gaap

manual car 手動汽車 sáu duhng hei chē

map 地圖 deih tòuh

market 市場 síh chèuhng

married 結咗婚 git jó fān

marry *v* 結婚 git fān

mass (church service) 禮拜 láih baai

massage 按摩 ngon mō

match *n* 火柴 fó chàaih

meal 飯 faahn

measure *v* (someone) 測量 chāak leuhng

measuring cup 量杯 lèuhng būi

measuring spoon 量羹 lèuhng gāng

mechanic 技工 geih gūng

medicine 醫藥 yī yeuhk

medium (size) 中等 jūng dáng

meet *v* (someone) 見面 gin mihn

meeting 會議 wuih yíh

meeting room 會議室 wuih yíh sāt

membership card 會員證 wúih yùhn jing

memorial (place) 紀念館 gei nihm gún

memory card 存儲卡 chyúh chyùhn kāat

mend *v* 修理 sāu léih

menstrual cramp 經期腹痛 gīng kèih fūk tung

menu 菜單 choi dāan

message 信息 seun sīk

microwave 微波爐 mèih bō lòuh

midday [BE] 晏晝 ngaan jau

midnight 午夜 ngh yeh

mileage 里數 léih sou

mini-bar 小酒吧 síu jáu bā

minute 分鐘 fān jūng

missing 錯過 cho gwo

mistake 差錯 chā cho

mobile phone [BE] 手提電話 sáu tàih dihn wá

mobility 流動性 làuh dung sing

monastery 修道院 sāu douh yún

money 錢 chín

month 月 yuht piu

mop 擦 chaat

moped 電單車 dihn dāan chē

more 多啲 dō dī

morning 早晨 jóu sàhn

mosque 清真寺 chīng jān jí

mother 媽媽 màh mā

motion sickness 暈浪 wàhn lohng

motor boat 汽船 hei syùhn

motorcycle 電單車 dihn dāan chē

motorway [BE] 高速公路 gōu chūk gūng louh

mountain 山 sāan

mountain bike 爬山電單車 pàh sāan dihn dāan chē

mouth 口 háu

movie 電影 dihn yíng

movie theater 電影院 dihn yíng yún

mug *v* 搶 chéung

multiple-trip (ticket) 無限次使用嘅 mòuh haahn chi sí yuhng ge

muscle 肌肉 gēi yuhk

museum 博物館 bok maht gún

music 音樂 yām ngohk

music store 音樂商店 yām ngohk sēung dim

N

nail file 指甲銼 jí gaap cho

name 名 méng

napkin 餐巾 chāan gān

nappy [BE] 尿片 niuh pín

nationality 國籍 gwok jihk

nature preserve 自然保護區 jih yìhn bóu wuh kēui

nauseous 想嘔 séung ngáu

near 附近 fuh gahn

near-sighted [BE] 近視 gahn sih

nearby 附近 fuh gahn

neck 頸 géng

necklace 頸鏈 géng lín

need v 需要 sēui yiu

newspaper 報紙 bou jí

newsstand 報攤 bou tāan

next 下一個 hah yāt go

nice 好 hóu

night 夜 yeh

nightclub 夜總會 yeh júng wúi

no 唔 m

non-alcoholic 無酒精 mòuh jáu jīng

non-smoking 禁煙 gam yīn

noon 中午 jūng bouh

north 北部 bāk bouh

nose 鼻 beih

nothing 冇乜野 móuh māt yéh

notify v 通知 tūng jī

novice (skill level) 新手 sān sáu

now 宜家 yìh gā

number 數字 sou jih

nurse 護士 wuh sih

O

office 辦公室 baahn gūng sāt

office hours 辦公時間 baahn gūng sìh gaan

off-license [BE] 酒店 jáu dim

oil 油 yàuh

OK 好 hóu

old 老 lóuh

one-way (ticket) 單程 dāan chìhng

one-way street 單程路 dāan chìhng louh

only 只係 jí haih

open v 打開 dá hōi; adj 開著 hōi jeuhk

opera 歌劇 gō kehk

opera house 歌劇院 gō kehk yún

opposite 相反 sēung fáan

optician 驗光師 yihm gwōng sī

orange (color) 橙 cháang

orchestra 管弦樂 gún yìhn ngohk

order v 叫野 giu yéh

outdoor pool 室外游泳池 sāt ngoih yàuh wihng chìh

outside 外面 ngoih mihn

overdone 太熟 taai suhk

overlook (scenic place) 俯視 fú sih

overnight 隔夜 gaahk yeh

oxygen treatment 氧氣治療 yéuhng hei jih lìuh

P

p.m. 下晝 hah jau

pacifier 奶嘴 náaih jéui

pack v 打包 dá bāau

package 包裹 bāau gwó

paddling pool [BE] 兒童泳池 yìh tùhng wihng chìh

pad [BE] (sanitary) 墊 jin

pain 痛 tung

pajamas 睡衣 seuih yī

palace 宮殿 gūng dihn

pants 褲 fu

pantyhose 絲襪 sī maht

paper 紙 jí

paper towel 紙巾 jí gān

park v 停車 tìhng chē; n 公園 gūng yún

parking garage 車房 chē fòhng

parking lot 停車場 tìhng chē chèuhng

parking meter 停車計時器 tìhng chē gai sìh hei

part-time 兼職 gīm jīk

passenger 乘客 sìhng haak

passport 護照 wuh jiu

passport control 護照管制 wuh jiu gún jai

password 密碼 maht máh

pastry shop 點心店 dím sām dim

path 道路 douh louh

pay v 支付 jī fuh

pay phone 公用電話 gūng yuhng dihn wá

peak (of a mountain) 山頂 sāan déng

pearl 珍珠 jān jyū

pedestrian 行人 hàahng yàhn

pediatrician 兒科醫生 yìh fō yī sāng

pedicure 修腳趾甲 sāu jín geuk gaap

pen 筆 bāt

per 每 múih

per day 每日 múih yaht

per hour 每個鐘頭 múih go jūng tàuh

per night 每晚 múih máahn

per week 每個星期 múih go sīng kèih

perfume 香水 hēung séui

period (menstrual) 月經 yuht gīng; **(of time)** 期間 kèih gāan

permit v 准 jéun

petite 嬌小 gīu síu

petrol [BE] 汽油 hei yàuh

petrol station [BE] 加油站 gā yàuh jaahm

pharmacy 藥房 yeuhk fòhng

phone v 打電話 dá dihn wá; n 電話 dihn wá

phone call 電話 dihn wá

phone card 電話卡 dihn wá kāat

phone number 電話號碼 dihn wá houh máh

photo 相 séung

photocopy 影印本 yíng yan bún

photography 影相 yíng séung

picnic area 野餐區 yéh chāan kēui

piece 塊 faai

pill (birth control) 避孕丸 beih yahn yún

pillow 枕頭 jám tàuh

personal identification number (PIN) 個人密碼 go yàhn maht máh

pink 粉紅色 fán hùhng sīk

piste [BE] 小路 síu louh

piste map [BE] 小路路線圖 síu louh louh sin tòuh

place v **(a bet)** 落 lohk

plane 飛機 fēi gēi

plastic wrap 塑膠包裝 sou gāau bāau jōng

plate 碟 díp

platform 月臺 yuht tòïh

platinum 鉑金 baahk gām

play v 玩 wáan; n **(theater)** 戲劇 hei kehk

playground 操場 chōu chèuhng

playpen 遊戲圍欄 yàuh hei wàih làahn

please 唔該 m gōi

pleasure 樂趣 lohk cheui

plunger 泵 bām

plus size 加大碼 gā daaih máh

pocket 袋 dói

poison 毒藥 duhk yeuhk

police 警察 gíng chaat

police report 警察報告 gíng chaat bou gou

police station 警察局 gíng chaat gúk

pond 池塘 chìh tóng

pool 水池 séui chìh

portion 部分 bouh fahn

post [BE] 郵件 yàuh gín

post office 郵局 yàuh gúk

postbox [BE] 郵箱 yàuh sēung

postcard 明信片 mìhn seun pín

pot 罐 gun

pottery 陶器 tòuh hei

pound (weight) 磅 bohng

pound (British sterling) 英鎊 yīng bóng

pregnant 有咗 yáuh jó

prescribe v 開處方 hōi chyúh fōng

prescription 處方藥 chyúh fōng yeuhk

press v (clothing) 熨 tong

price 價格 ga gaak

print v 列印 liht yan

problem 問題 mahn tàih

produce 農產品 nùhng cháan bán

produce store 農產品商店 nùhng cháan bán sēung dim

prohibit v 禁止 gam jí

pronounce v 發音 faat yām

public 公共 gūng guhng

pull v 拉 lāai

purple 紫色 jí sīk

purse 銀包 ngàhn bāau

push v 按 ngon

pushchair [BE] BB車 bìhbī chē

Q

quality 質量 jāt leuhng

question 問題 mahn tàih

quiet 安靜 ngōn jihng

R

racetrack 跑馬場 páau máh chèuhng

racket (sports) 球拍 kàuh páak

railway station [BE] 火車 fó chē

rain 雨 yúh

raincoat 雨褸 yúh lāu

rainforest 雨林 yúh làhm

rainy 多雨 dō yúh

rap (music) 說唱樂 syut cheung lohk

rape 強姦 kèuhng gāan

rare (object) 罕見 hón gin

rash 疹 chán

ravine 峽谷 haap gūk

razor blade 剃鬚刀 tai sōu dōu

reach v 到 dou

ready 準備好 jéun beih hóu

real 真正 jān jing

receipt 收據 sāu geui

receive v 接受 jip sauh

reception 招待會 jīu doih wúi

recharge v 充電 chūng dihn

recommend v 介紹 gaai siuh

recommendation 推薦 tēui jin

recycling 回收 wùih sāu

red 紅色 hùhng sīk

refrigerator 冰箱 bīng sēung

region 區域 kēui wihk

registered mail 掛號信 gwa houh seun

regular 普通 pōu tūng

relationship 關係 gwāan haih

Ren Min Bi (Chinese currency) 人民幣 yàhn màhn baih

rent v 租 jōu

rental car 的士 dīk sí

repair v 修理 sāu léih

repeat v 重複 chùhng fūk

reservation 預定 yuh dihng

reservation desk 服務台 fuhk mouh tòih

reserve v 預定 yuh dehng

restaurant 餐館 chāan gún

restroom 休息室 yāu sīk sāt

retired 退休 teui yāu

return v 還 wàahn

return (ticket) 雙程 sēung chìhng

reverse v (the charges) [BE] 對方付費電話 deui fōng fuh fai dihn wá

rib (body part) 肋骨 laahk gwāt

rice cooker 電飯煲 dihn faahn bōu

right of way 路權 louh kyùhn

ring 戒指 gaai jí

river 河 hòh

road map 路線圖 louh sin tòuh

roast v 烤 hāau

rob v 搶奪 chéung dyuht

robbed 畀人搶野 béi yàhn chéung yéh

romantic 浪漫 lohng maahn

room 房間 fòhng gāan

room key 房間鎖匙 fòhng gāan só sìh

room service 客房送餐服務 haak fóng sung chāan fuhk mouh

round-trip 雙程 sēung chìhng

route 路線 louh sin

rowboat 扒艇 pàh téhng

rubbish [BE] 垃圾 laahp saap

rubbish bag [BE] 垃圾袋 laahp saap dói

ruins 廢墟 fai hēui

rush 趕時間 gón sìh gaan

S

sad 傷心 sēung sām

safe (storage) 保險箱 bóu hím sēung; **(protected)** 安全 ngōn chyùhn

sales tax 銷售稅 sīu sauh seui

same 同一 tùhng yāt

sandals 涼鞋 lèuhng hàaih

sanitary napkin 衛生棉 waih sāng mìhn

saucepan 平底鑊 pìhng dái wohk

sauna 桑拿 sōng nàh

save v **(on a computer)** 保存 bóu chyùhn

savings (account) 儲蓄 chyúh chūk

scanner 掃描器 sou mìuh hei

scarf 絲巾 sī gān

schedule v 預定日程 yuh dihng yaht chìhng; n 日程表 syaht chìhng bíu

school 學校 hohk haauh

scissors 較剪 gaau jín

sea 海 hói

seat 座位 joh wái

security 保安 bóu ngōn

see v 睇見 tái gin

self-service 自助 jih joh

sell v 賣 maaih

seminar 研討會 yìhng tóu wúi

send v 送 sung

senior citizen 老年人 lóuh nìhn yàhn

separated (marriage) 分居 fān gēui

serious 嚴肅 yìhm sūk

service (in a restaurant) 服務 fuhk mouh

shampoo 洗頭水 sái tàuh séui

sharp 利 leih

shaving cream 剃鬚膏 tai sōu gōu

sheet 床單 chòhng dāan

ship v **(mail)** 運送 wahn sung

shirt 恤衫 sēut sāam

shoe store 鞋鋪 hàaih póu

shoes 鞋 hàaih

shop v 買野 máaih yéh

shopping 購物 kau maht

shopping area 購物區 kau maht kēui

shopping centre [BE] 商場 sēung chèuhng

shopping mall 商場 sēung chèuhng

short 短 dyún

short sleeves 短袖 dyún jauh

shorts 短褲 dyún fu

short-sighted [BE] 近視 gahn sih

shoulder 膊頭 bok tàuh

show v 顯示 hín sih

shower 沖涼 chūng lèuhng

shrine 寺廟 jih míu

sick 病 behng

side dish 配菜 pui choi

side effect 副作用 fu jok yuhng

sightseeing 觀光 gūn gwōng

sightseeing tour 觀光旅遊 gūn gwōng léuih yàuh

sign v 簽名 chīm méng

silk 絲綢 sī chàuh

silver 銀 ngàhn

single (unmarried) 單身 dāan sān

single bed 單人床 dāan yàhn chòhng

single room 單人房間 dāan yàhn fóng

sink 瓷盆 chìh pùhn

sister 姐妹 jí múi

sit v 坐低 chóh dāi

size 尺寸 chek chyun

skin 皮膚 pèih fū

skirt 裙 kwàhn

sleep v 訓覺 fan gaau

sleeper car 臥鋪車 ngoh pōu chē

sleeping bag 睡袋 seuih dói

sleeping car [BE] 臥鋪車 ngoh pōu chē

slice (of something) 片 pin

slippers 拖鞋 tō háai

slowly 慢慢地 maahn máan déi

small 小 síu

smoke v 食煙 sihk yīn

smoking (area) 食煙 sihk yīn

snack bar 小食店 síu sihk dim

sneaker 運動鞋 wahn duhn hàaih

snorkeling equipment 水底呼吸設備 séui dái fū kāp chit beih

soap 番鹼 fāan gáan

soccer 足球 jūk kàuh

sock 襪 maht

soother [BE] 奶嘴 náaih jéui

sore throat 喉嚨痛 hàuh lùhng tung

sorry 抱歉 póu hip

south 南 nàahm

souvenir 紀念品 gei nihm bán

souvenir store 紀念品商店 gei nihm bán sēung dim

spa 溫泉 wān chyùhn

spatula 鏟 cháan

speak v 講 góng

specialist (doctor) 專家 jyūn gā

specimen 標本 bīu bún

speeding 超速 chīu chūk

spell v 串 chyun

spicy 辣 laaht

spine (body part) 脊椎 bui jēui

spoon 匙羹 chìh gāng

sports 體育 tái yuhk

sporting goods store 體育用品 商店 tái yuhk yuhng bán sēung dim

sports massage 按摩 ngon mō

sprain 扭傷 náu sēung

stadium 體育場 tái yuhk chèuhng

stairs 樓梯 làuh tāi

stamp v (a ticket) 蓋印 koi yan; n (postage) 郵票 yàuh piu

start v 開始 hōi chíh

starter [BE] 開胃菜 hōi waih choi

station 站 jaahm

statue 雕像 dīu jeuhng

stay v 住喺 jyuh hái

steal v 偷 tāu

steamer 蒸鍋 jīng wō

steep 斜 che

sterling silver 純銀 syùhn ngán

stewed 燉 dahn

stolen 畀人偷咗 béi yàhn tāu jó

stomach 胃 waih

stomachache 胃痛 waih tung

stop v 停低 tìhng dāi; n 站 jaahm

store directory 商店目錄 sēung dim muhk luhk

storey [BE] 層 chàhng

stove 爐 lòuh

straight 直 jihk

strange 奇怪 kèih gwaai

stream 小溪 síu kāi

stroller BB 車 bìh bī chē

student 學生 hohk sāang

study v 學習 hohk jaahp

stunning 震驚 jan gīng

subtitle 副標題 fu bīu tàih

subway 地鐵 deih tit

subway station 地鐵站 deih tit jaahm

suit 西服套裝 sāi fuhk tou jōng

suitcase 手提箱 sáu tàih sēung

sun 太陽 taai yèuhng

sunblock 防曬霜 fòhng saai sēung

sunburn 曬傷 saai sēung

sunglasses 太陽眼鏡 taai yèuhng ngáahn géng

sunny 晴朗 chìhng lóhng

sunscreen 防曬霜 fòhng saai sēung

sunstroke 中暑 jung syú

super (fuel) 超級 chīu kāp

supermarket 超級市場 chīu kāp síh chèuhng

supervision 監督 gāam d zenask

surfboard 滑浪板 waaht lohng báan

swallow v 吞 tān

sweater 毛衣 mòuh yī

sweatshirt 運動衫 wahn duhng sāam

sweet (taste) 甜 tìhm

swelling 腫 júng

swim v 游水 yàuh séui

swimsuit 泳衣 wihng yī

symbol (keyboard) 標誌 bīu ji

synagogue 猶太教堂 yàuh taai gaau tóng

table 檯 tói

tablet (medicine) 藥丸 yeuhk yún

take v 食藥 sihk yeuhk

take away [BE] 摞走 ló jáu

tampon 棉條 mìhn tíu

taste v 試吓 si háh

taxi 的士 dīk sí

team 隊 déui

teahouse 茶樓 chàh làuh

teaspoon 茶匙 chàh chìh

telephone 電話 dihn wá

temple (religious) 寺廟 jíh míu

temporary 臨時 làhm sih

tennis 網球 móhng kàuh

tent 帳篷 jeung fùhng

tent peg 帳蓬樁 jeung fùhng jōng

tent pole 帳篷杆 jeung fùhng gōn

terminal (airport) 候機大堂 hauh gēi daaih tòhng

terrible 可怕 hó pa

text *v* (send a message) 發短信 faat dyún seun; *n* (message) 文字 màhn jih

thank *v* 感謝 gám jeh

thank you 多謝 dō jeh

that 嗰 gó

theater 戲院 hei yún

theft 偷竊 tāu sit

there 嗰度 gó douh

thief 賊 cháak

thigh 大腿 daaih téui

thirsty 口渴 háu hot

this 呢 nī

throat 喉嚨 hàuh lùhng

thunderstorm 雷雨 lèuih yúh

ticket 票 piu

ticket office 售票處 sauh piu chyu

tie (clothing) 領呔 léhng tāai

tights [BE] 絲襪 sī maht

time 時間 sìh gaan

timetable [BE] 時間表 sìh gaan bíu

tire 車胎 chē tāai

tired 癐喇 guih la

tissue 紙巾 jí gān

to go 去 heui

tobacconist 煙草零售商 yīn chóu lìhng sauh sēung

today 今日 gām yaht

toe 腳趾 geuk jí

toenail 趾甲 jí gaap

toilet [BE] 沖涼房 chūng lèuhng fóng

toilet paper 廁紙 chi jí

tomorrow 聽日 tīng yaht

tongue 舌 siht

tonight 今晚 gām máahn

too 太 taai

tooth 牙 ngàh

toothpaste 牙膏 ngàh gōu

total (amount) 一共 yāt guhng

tourist 旅客 léuih haak

tourist information office 旅遊資訊辦公室 léuih yàuh jī seun baahn gūng sāt

tour 遊覽 yàuh láahm

tow truck 拖車 tō chē

towel 毛巾 mòuh gān

tower 塔 taap

town 鎮 jan

town hall 市政廳 síh jing tēng

town map 市地圖 síh deih tòuh

town square 市中心廣場 síh jūng sām gwóng chèuhng

toy 玩具 wuhn geuih

toy store 玩具店 wuhn geui dim

track (train) 鐵軌 tit gwái

traditional 傳統 chyùhn túng

traffic light 紅綠燈 hùhng luhk dāng

trail 山路小徑 sāan louh síu ging

trail map 山路圖 sāan louh tòuh

train 火車 fó chē

train station 火車站 fó chē jaahm

transfer v (change trains/ flights) 轉 jyun; v (money) 轉賬 jyún jeung

translate v 翻譯 fāan yihk

trash 垃圾 laahp saap

travel agency 旅行社 léuih hàhng séh

travel sickness 暈浪 wàhn lohng

traveler's check 旅行支票 léuih hàhng jī piu

traveller's cheque [BE] 旅行支票 léuih hàhng jī piu

tree 樹 syuh

trim (hair cut) 剪 jín

trip 旅程 léuih chìhng

trolley [BE] 電車 dihn chē

trousers [BE] 長褲 chèuhng fu

T-shirt T恤 tī sēut

turn off (lights) 熄 sīk

turn on (lights) 開 hōi

TV 電視 dihn sih

type v 打字 dá jih

U

ugly 難睇 nàahn tái

umbrella 遮 jē

unattended 無人睇 móuh yàhn tái

unconscious 冇知覺 móuh jī gok

underground [BE] 地下 deih há

underground station [BE] 地鐵站 deih tit jaahm

understand v 理解 léih gáai

underwear 底衫 dái sāam

unemployed 失業者 sāt yihp jé

United Kingdom (U.K.) 英國 yīng gwok

United States (U.S.) 美國 méih gwok

university 大學 daaih hohk

unleaded (gas) 無鉛 mòuh yùhn

upper 上部 seuhng bouh

upset stomach 腸胃不適 chèuhng waih bāt sīk

urgent 緊急 gán gāp

urine 尿 niuh

use v 使用 sí yuhng

username 用戶名 yuhng wuh méng

utensil 器皿 hei míhng

V

vacancy 有空房 yáuh hūng fóng

vacation 假期 ga kèih

vaccination 防疫 fòhng yihk

vacuum cleaner 吸塵器 kāp chàhn hei

vagina 陰道 yām douh

vaginal infection 陰道傳染 yām douh chyùhn yíhm

valid 合法 hahp faat

valley 河谷 hòh gūk

valuable 貴重嘅 gwai juhng ge

value 價值 ga jihk

vegetarian 素食者 sou sihk jé

vehicle registration 車輛註冊 chē léuhng jyu chaak

viewpoint [BE] 觀點 gūn dím

village 村莊 chyūn jōng

vineyard 葡萄園 pòuh tòuh yùhn

visa 簽證 chīm jing

visit v 參觀 chāam gūn

visiting hours 探病時間 taam behng sìh gaan

visually impaired 弱視者 yeuhk sih jé

vitamin 維生素 wàih sāng sou

V-neck V 領 wī léhng

volleyball game 排球賽 pàaih kàuh choi

vomit v 嘔 ngáu

W

wait v 等 dáng; n 等候時間 dáng hauh sìh gaan

waiter 服務員 fuhk mouh yùhn

waiting room 候診室 hauh chán sāt

waitress 女服務員 néuih fuhk mouh yùhn

wake v 醒 séng

wake-up call 叫醒服務 giu séng fuhk mouh

walk v 走 jáu; n 步行 bouh hàhng

walking route 步行路線 bouh hàhng louh sin

wall clock 掛鐘 gwa jūng

wallet 銀包 ngàhn bāau

war memorial 戰爭紀念館 jin jāng gei nihm gún

warm adj/v 暖 nyúhn

washing machine 洗衣機 sái yī gēi

watch 手錶 sáu bīu

water skis 滑水板 waaht séui báan

waterfall 瀑布 bohk bou

weather 天氣 tīn hei

week 星期 sīng kèih

weekend 週末 jāu muht

weekly 每週 múih jāu

welcome v 歡迎 fūn yìhng

well-rested 休息得好好 yāu sīk dāk hóu hóu

west 西部 sāi bouh

what 乜野 māt yéh

wheelchair 輪椅 lèuhn yí

wheelchair ramp 輪椅道 lèuhn yí douh

when 幾時 géi sìh

where 邊度 bīn douh

white 白色 baahk sīk

who 邊個 bīn go

wife 老婆 lóuh pòh

window 窗 chēung

window case 櫥窗 chyùhn chēung

wine list 酒類表 jáu leuih bíu

wireless internet 無線互聯網 mòuh sin wuh lyùhn móhng

wireless internet service 無線互聯網服務 mòuh sin wuh lyùhn móhng fuhk mouh

wireless phone 無線電話 mòuh sin dihn wá

with 同 tùhng

withdraw v 退出 teui chēut

withdrawal (bank) 取錢 chéui chín

without 冇 móuh

wok 炒鍋 sō wō

woman 女人 néuih yán

wool 羊毛 yèuhng mòuh

work v 做野 jouh yéh

wrap v (a package) 包 bāau

wrist 手腕 sáu wún

write v 寫 sé

Y

year 年 nìhn

yellow 黃色 wòhng sīk

yes 係 haih

yesterday 琴日 kàhm yaht

young 年輕 nìhn hīng

youth hostel 青年旅舍 chīng nìhn léuih se

Z

zoo 動物園 duhng maht yùhn

Chinese–English Dictionary

A

阿斯匹零 **a sī pāt lìhng** aspirin

B

芭蕾 **bā lèuih** ballet

巴士 **bā sí** bus

巴士車票 **bā sí chē piu** bus ticket

巴士站 **bā sí jaahm** bus station; bus stop

巴士遊覽 **bā sí yàuh láahm** bus tour

鉑金 **baahk gām** platinum

白色 **baahk sīk** white

辦公室 **baahn gūng sāt** office

辦公時間 **baahn gūng sìh gaan** office hours

辦理登機手續 **baahn léih dāng gēi sáu juhk** check-in (airport)

百貨公司 **baak fo gūng sī** department store

包 **bāau** v wrap (a package)

包裹 **bāau gwó** package

包括 **bāau kwut** v include

北部 **bāk bouh** north

泵 **bām** plunger

繃帶 **bāng dáai** bandage

筆 **bāt** pen

病 **behng** sick [ill BE]

畀 **béi** v give

比較少 **béi gaau síu** less

比基尼裝 **béi gīn nèih jōng** bikini

畀人搶嘢 **béi yàhn chéung yéh** robbed

畀人偷咗 **béi yàhn tāu jó** stolen

鼻 **beih** nose

避孕丸 **beih yahn yún** pill (birth control)

避孕套 **beih yan tou** condom

BB **bìh bī** baby

BB車 **bìhbī chē** stroller [pushchair BE]

邊度 **bīn douh** where

邊個 **bīn go** who

便秘 **bin bei** constipated

變壓器 **bin ngaat hei** adapter

冰 **bīng** ice

冰球 **bīng kàuh** ice hockey

冰冷 **bīng láahng** icy

冰箱 **bīng sēung** refrigerator

標本 **bīu bún** specimen

表格 **bíu gaak** form (fill-in)

標誌 **bīu ji** symbol (keyboard)

玻璃 **bō lēi** glass (material)

玻璃杯 **bō lēi būi** glass (drinking)

瀑布 **bohk bou** waterfall

磅 **bohng** pound (weight)

博物館 **bok maht gún** museum

膊頭 **bok tàuh** shoulder

幫助 **bōng joh** help

保存 **bóu chyùhn** v save (on a computer)

保險 **bóu hím** insurance

保險公司 **bóu hím gūng sī** insurance company

保險卡 **bóu hím kāat** insurance card

保險箱 **bóu hím sēung** safe (storage)

保姆 **bóu móuh** babysitter

保安 **bóu ngōn** security

保鮮紙 **bóu sīn jí** plastic wrap [cling film BE]

報紙 **bou jí** newspaper

報攤 **bou tāan** newsstand

部分 **bouh fahn** portion

曝光 **bouh gwōng** exposure (film)

步行 **bouh hàhng** n walk

步行路線 **bouh hàhng louh sin** walking route

撥號 **buht houh** v dial

杯 **būi** cup

背脊 **bui jek** back (body part)

脊椎 **bui jēui** spine (body part)

背囊 **bui nòhng** backpack

背痛 **bui tung** backache

半 **bun** half

半公斤 **bun gūng gān** half-kilo

半小時 **bun síu sìh** half hour

叉 **chā** fork

差錯 **chā cho** mistake

殘疾 **chàahn jaht** disabled; handicapped

殘疾人通道 **chàahn jaht yàhn tūng douh** hadicapped [disabled BE] accessible

踩單車 **cháai dāan chē** cycling

賊 **cháak** thief

測量 **chāak leuhng** v measure (someone)

參觀 **chāam gūn** v visit

鏟 **cháan** spatula

餐巾 **chāan gān** napkin

餐館 **chāan gún** restaurant

橙 **cháang** orange (color)

插入 **chaap yahp** v insert (on an ATM)

擦 **chaat** mop

茶匙 **chàh chìh** teaspoon

茶樓 **chàh làuh** teahouse

陳列櫃 **chàhn liht gwaih** display case

柴油 **chàih yàuh** diesel

疹 **chán** rash

漆器 **chāt hei** lacquerware

斜 **che** steep

車房 **chē fòhng** parking garage

車輛註冊 **chē léuhng jyu chaak** vehicle registration

車胎 **chē tāai** tire [tyre BE]

尺寸 **chek chyun** size

長 **chèuhng** long

長褲 **chèuhng fu** pants [trousers BE]

長袖 **chèuhng jauh** long sleeves

長筒襪 **chèuhng túng maht** tight

腸胃不適 **chèuhng waih bāt sīk** upset stomach

錘 **chéui** hammer

取錢 **chéui chín** withdrawal (bank)

取消 **chéui sīu** v cancel

搶 **chéung** v mug

腸 **chéung** intestine

窗 **chēung** window

搶奪 **chéung dyuht** v rob

出口 **chēut háu** n exit

出去 **chēut heui** v exit

出席 **chēut jihk** v attend

出租汽車 **chēut jōu hei chē** car rental [hire BE]

出納員 **chēut naahp yùhn** cashier

廁紙 **chi jí** toilet paper

遲啲 **chìh dī** v delay

匙羹 **chìh gāng** spoon

瓷器 **chìh hei** china

遲咗 **chìh jó** late (time)

瓷盆 **chìh pùhn** sink

池塘 **chìh tòng** pond

潛水 **chìhm séui** v dive

潛水用具 **chìhm séui yuhng geuih** diving equipment

晴朗 **chìhng lóhng** sunny

簽證 **chīm jing** visa

簽名 **chīm méng** v sign

錢 **chín** money

清除 **chīng chèuih** v clear (on an ATM)

清潔產品 **chīng git cháan bán** cleaning product

清真寺 **chīng jān jí** mosque

清真食品 **chīng jān sihk bán** halal

青年旅舍 **chīng nìhn léuih se** youth hostel

設備 **chit beih** equipment

超速 **chīu chūk** speeding

超過 **chīu gwo** excess

超級 **chīu kāp** super (fuel)

超級市場 **chīu kāp síh chèuhng** supermarket

錯過 **cho gwo** missing

初學者 **chō hohk jé** beginner (skill level)

坐低 **chóh dāi** v sit

床 **chòhng** bed

床單 **chòhng dāan** sheet

床仔 **chòhng jái** cot

菜單 **choi dāan** menu

艙 **chōng** class

闖入 **chóng yahp** break-in (burglary)

操場 **chōu chèuhng** playground

蟲 **chùhng** bug

重複 **chùhng fūk** v repeat

蟲咬 **chùhng ngáau** insect bite

充電 **chūng dihn** v recharge

充血 **chūng hyut** congestion

沖涼 **chūng lèuhng** shower

櫥窗 **chyùh chēung** window case

儲蓄 **chyúh chūk** n deposit (bank); savings (account)

存儲卡 **chyúh chyùhn kāat** memory card

廚房 **chyùh fóng** kitchen

廚房錫紙 **chyùh fóng sehk jí** aluminum [kitchen BE] foil

處方藥 **chyúh fōng yeuhk** prescription

存錢 **chyùhn chín** v deposit

傳真 **chyùhn jān** n fax

傳真號碼 **chyùhn jān houh máh** fax number

傳統 **chyùhn túng** traditional

傳染 **chyùhn yíhm** infected

傳染嘅 **chyùhn yíhm ge** contagious

串 **chyun** v spell

村莊 **chyūn jōng** village

打包 **dá bāau** v pack

打電話 **dá dihn wá** v call; phone

打火機 **dá fó gēi** lighter

打擾 **dá gáau** v bother

打開 **dá hōi** v open

打字 **dá jih** v type

帶嚟 **daai làih** v bring

大 **daaih** large

大教堂 **daaih gaau tòhng** cathedral

大廈 **daaih hah** building

大學 **daaih hohk** university

大腿 **daaih tēui** thigh

單 **dāan** n bill (of sale)

單車 **dāan chē** bicycle

單車路線 **dāan chē louh sin** bike route

單程 **dāan chìhng** one-way (ticket)

單程路 **dāan chìhng louh** one-way street

單獨 **dāan duhk** alone

單身 **dāan sān** single (unmarried)

單人床 **dāan yàhn chòhng** single bed

單人房間 **dāan yàhn fóng** single room

搭車 **daap chē** v hitchhike

燉 **dahn** stewed

低 **dāi** low

抵達 **dái daaht** arrivals (airport)

底衫 **dái sāam** underwear

第一 **daih yāt** first

得意 **dāk yi** cute

凳 **dang** chair

等 **dáng** v wait

燈 **dāng** light (overhead)

燈膽 **dāng dáam** lightbulb

登機 **dāng gēi** v board

登機証 **dāng gēi jing** boarding pass

登機門 **dāng gēi mùhn** gate [airport]

等候時間 **dáng hauh sìh gaan** n wait

登錄 **dāng luhk** log on

地板 **deih báan** floor

地址 **deih jí** address

地鐵 **deih tit** subway [underground BE]

地鐵站 **deih tit jaahm** subway station [underground BE]

地圖 **deih tòuh** map

隊 **déui** team

對方付費電話 **deui fōng fuh fai dihn wá** v call collect [reverse the charges BE]

兌換 **deui wuhn** v exchange (money)

兌換率 **deui wuhn léut** exchange rate

DVD **dī wī dī** DVD

滴 **dihk** drop (medicine)

電車 **dihn chē** tram

電單車 **dihn dāan chē** motorcycle

電飯煲 **dihn faahn bōu** rice cooker

電風扇 **dihn fūng sin** fan (appliance)

電制 **dihn jai** electric outlet

電子票 **dihn jí piu** e-ticket

電子郵件 **dihn jí yàuh gín** n e-mail

電腦 **dihn nóuh** computer

電芯 **dihn sām** battery

電視 **dihn sih** TV

電梯 **dihn tāi** lift [elevator BE]

電筒 **dihn túng** flashlight

電話 **dihn wá** n call; phone call; telephone

電話號碼 **dihn wá houh máh** phone number

電話卡 **dihn wá kāat** phone card

電郵地址 **dihn yàuh deih jí** e-mail address

電影 **dihn yíng** movie

電影院 **dihn yíng yún** movie theater

碟 **dihp** dish (kitchen)

的士 **dīk sí** taxi

點 **dím** light (cigarette)

點心店 **dím sām dim** pastry shop

點樣 **dím yéung** how

癲癇 **dīn gáan** epileptic

碟 **díp** plate

雕刻 **dīu hāk** *v* engrave

雕像 **dīu jeuhng** statue

吊車 **diu chē** drag lift

多啲 **dō dī** more

多謝 **dō jeh** thank you

多雨 **dō yúh** rainy

袋 **dói** bag; pocket

代辦處 **doih baahn chyu** agency

當地 **dōng deih** local

刀 **dōu** knife

賭場 **dóu chèuhng** casino

倒空 **dóu hūng** *v* empty

到 **dou** get to; *v* reach

到達 **dou daaht** *v* arrive

度 **douh** degrees (temperature)

渡輪 **douh lèuhn** ferry

道路 **douh louh** path

導盲犬 **douh màahng hyún** guide dog

毒藥 **duhk yeuhk** poison

動脈 **duhng mahk** artery

動物 **duhng maht** animal

動物園 **duhng maht yùhn** zoo

東部 **dūng bouh** east

短 **dyún** short

短褲 **dyún fu** shorts

短袖 **dyún jauh** short sleeves

F

花 **fā** flower

化妝乳液 **fa jōng yúh yihk** lotion

飯 **faahn** meal

飯廳 **faahn tēng** dining room

快 **faai** express

塊 **faai** piece

快餐 **faai chāan** fast food

快速 **faai chūk** fast

筷子 **faai jí** chopsticks

番檢 **fāan gáan** soap

翻譯 **fāan yihk** *v* translate

發傳真 **faat chyùhn jān** *v* fax

發電郵 **faat dihn yàuh** *v* e-mail

發短信 **faat dyún seun** *v* text (send a message)

發貨單 **faat fo dāan** invoice

琺瑯 **faat lòhng** enamel (jewelry)

髮廊 **faat lòhng** hair salon

發燒 **faat sīu** fever

發音 **faat yām** *v* pronounce

髮型 **faat yìhng** hairstyle

髮型師 **faat yìhng sī** hairstylist

罰款 **faht fún** fine (fee)

肺 **fai** lung

廢墟 **fai hēui** ruins

費用 **fai yuhng** fee

花粉症 **fān fán jing** hay fever

分機 **fān gēi** extension (phone)

分居 **fān gēui** separated (marriage)

分鐘 **fān jūng** minute

粉紅色 **fán hùhng sīk** pink

訓覺 **fan gaau** v sleep

飛髮 **fēi faat** haircut

飛機 **fēi gēi** airplane

飛機場 **fēi gēi chèuhng** airport

菲林 **fēi lám** film (camera)

火 **fó** fire

火柴 **fó chàaih** n match

火車 **fó chē** train

火車站 **fó chē jaahm** train [railway BE] station

貨幣 **fo baih** currency

貨幣兌換 **fo baih deui wuhn** currency exchange

貨幣兌換局 **fo baih deui wuhn gúk** currency exchange office

課程 **fo chìhng** lesson

防火門 **fòhng fó mùhn** fire door

房間 **fòhng gāan** room

房間鎖匙 **fòhng gāan só sìh** room key

防曬霜 **fòhng saai sēung** sunblock

防疫 **fòhng yihk** vaccination

方向 **fōng heung** direction

褲 **fu** pants

呼吸 **fū kāp** v breathe

俯視 **fú sih** overlook (scenic place)

副標題 **fu bīu tàih** subtitle

副作用 **fu jok yuhng** side effect

婦產科醫生 **fúh cháan fō yī sāng** gynecologist

父親 **fuh chān** father

附加費 **fuh gā fai** cover charge

附近 **fuh gahn** near; nearby

服裝要求 **fuhk jōng yīu kàuh** dress code

服務 **fuhk mouh** service (in a restaurant)

服務台 **fuhk mouh tòih** reservation desk

服務員 **fuhk mouh yùhn** waiter

灰色 **fūi sīk** gray

歡迎 **fūn yìhng** v welcome

風筒 **fūng túng** hair dryer

G

加大碼 **gā daaih máh** extra large

加滿 **gā múhn** v fill up (food)

家庭 **gā tìhng** family

加入 **gā yahp** v join

加油站 **gā yàuh jaahm** gas [petrol BE] station

加熱　**gā yiht** heat

加熱器　**gā yiht hei** heater

假牙　**gá ngàh** denture

咖啡店　**ga fē dìm** coffee shop

咖啡館　**ga fē gún** cafe

咖啡色　**ga fē sīk** brown

價格　**ga gaak** price

價格固定嘅菜單　**ga gaak gu dihng ge choi dāan** fixed-price menu

價值　**ga jihk** value

假期　**ga kèih** vacation [holiday BE]

加拿大　**ga nàh daaih** Canada

駕駛執照號碼　**ga sái jāp jiu houh máh** driver's license number

隔夜　**gaahk yeh** overnight

戒指　**gaai jí** ring

介紹　**gaai siuh** *v* introduce

監督　**gāam dūk** supervision

交換　**gāau wuhn** *v* exchange (goods)

較剪　**gaau jín** scissors

教堂　**gaau tóng** church

近視　**gahn sih** near-sighted [short-sighted BE]

計時器　**gai sìh hei** meter (parking)

金　**gām** gold

今晚　**gām máahn** tonight

感謝　**gám jeh** *v* thank

感冒　**gám mouh** cold (sickness)

今日　**gām yaht** today

禁止　**gam jí** *v* prohibit

禁煙　**gam yīn** non-smoking

緊急　**gán gāp** urgent

緊急出口　**gán gāp chēut háu** emergency exit

緊急狀態　**gán gāp johng taai** emergency

緊身褲　**gán sān fu** briefs (clothing)

更改路線　**gāng gói louh sin** alternate route

救生衣　**gau sāng yī** life jacket

救生員　**gau sāng yùhn** lifeguard

救護車　**gau sēung chē** ambulance

肌肉　**gēi yuhk** muscle

幾多　**géi dō** how much

幾時　**géi sìh** when

紀念品　**gei nihm bán** souvenir

紀念品商店　**gei nihm bán sēung dim** souvenir store

紀念館　**gei nihm gún** memorial (place)

技工　**geih gūng** mechanic

頸　**géng** neck

頸鏈　**géng lín** necklace

鏡片　**geng pín** lens

腳趾　**geui jí** toe

腳　**geuk** foot

腳眼 **geuk ngáahn** ankle

件 **gihn** case (amount)

健康 **gihn hōng** health

健康食品店 **gihn hōng sihk bán dim** health food store

檢查 **gím chàh** v check (something)

兼職 **gīm jīk** part-time

見面 **gin mihn** v meet (someone)

警察 **gíng chaat** police

警察報告 **gíng chaat bou gou** police report

警察局 **gíng chaat gúk** police station

經濟艙 **gīng jai chōng** economy class

經期腹痛 **gīng kèih fūk tung** menstrual cramp

經理 **gīng léih** manager

景泰藍 **gíng taai làahm** cloisonné

結束 **git chūk** v end

結婚 **git fān** v marry

嬌小 **gīu síu** petite

叫醒服務 **giu séng fuhk mouh** wake-up call

叫野 **giu yéh** v order

歌劇 **gō kehk** opera

歌劇院 **gō kehk yún** opera house

嗰 **gó** that

嗰度 **gó douh** there

個人密碼 **go yàhn maht máh** personal identification number (PIN)

改 **gói** v alter (clothing)

乾淨 **gōn jehng** adj clean

肝臟 **gōn johng** liver (body part)

乾洗店 **gōn sái dim** dry cleaner

趕時間 **gón sìh gaan** rush

講 **góng** v speak

港元 **góng yùhn** dollar (H.K.)

高 **gōu** high

高速公路 **gōu chūk gūng louh** highway [motorway BE]

高腳椅 **gōu geuk yí** highchair

高爾夫球比賽 **gōu yíh fū kàuh béi choi** golf tournament

高爾夫球場 **gōu yíh fū kàuh chèuhng** golf course

古典音樂 **gú dím yām ngohk** classical music

古董店 **gú dúng dim** antiques store

古龍水 **gú lùhng séui** cologne

故障 **gu jeung** breakdown

顧問 **gu mahn** consultant

雇用 **gu yuhng** v hire

瘡喇 **guih la** tired

罐 **gun** pot

觀點 **gūn dím** overlook [viewpoint BE]

觀光 **gūn gwōng** sightseeing

觀光旅遊 **gūn gwōng léuih yàuh** sightseeing tour

宮殿 **gūng dihn** palace

公斤 **gūng gān** kilogram

攻擊 **gūng gīk** attack (on person)

公共 **gūng guhng** public

公仔 **gūng jái** doll

公里 **gūng léih** kilometer

公升 **gūng sīng** liter

公寓 **gūng yuh** apartment

公用電話 **gūng yuhng dihn wá** pay phone

公園 **gūng yún** *n* park

掛號信 **gwa houh seun** registered mail

掛鐘 **gwa jūng** wall clock

關閉 **gwāan bai** closed

關係 **gwāan haih** relationship

關節 **gwāan jit** joint (body part)

關節炎 **gwāan jit yìhm** arthritis

關門 **gwāan mùhn** *v* close (a shop)

關稅 **gwāan seui** duty (tax)

貴重嘅 **gwai juhng ge** valuable

骨頭 **gwāt tàuh** bone

過敏反應 **gwo máhn fáan ying** allergic reaction

國家代號 **gwok gā doih houh** country code

國際 **gwok jai** international (airport area)

國際學生證 **gwok jai hohk sāang jing** international student card

國際航班 **gwok jai hòhng bāan** international flight

國籍 **gwok jihk** nationality

國內 **gwok noih** domestic

國內航班 **gwok noih hòhng bāan** domestic flight

H

行人 **hàahng yàhn** pedestrian

鞋 **hàaih** shoes

鞋帶 **hàaih dáai** lace

鞋鋪 **hàaih póu** shoe store

客艙 **haak chōng** cabin

客房清潔服務 **haak fóng chīng git fuhk móuh** housekeeping services

客房送餐服務 **haak fóng sung chāan fuhk mouh** room service

峽谷 **haap gūk** ravine

烤 **hāau** *v* roast

烤肉 **hāau yuhk** barbecue

下晝 **hah jau** afternoon; p.m.

下爬 **hah pàh** jaw

下一個 **hah yāt go** next

行李 **hàhng léih** luggage

行李車 **hàhng léih chē** cart (luggage)

行李暫存箱 **hàhng léih jaahm chyùhn sēung** luggage locker

行李票 hàhng léih piu luggage [baggage BE] ticket
行李推車 hàhng léih tēui chē luggage cart [trolley BE]
行李認領 hàhng léih yihng léhng baggage claim
合法 hahp faat valid
喺 hái in
係 haih yes
克 hāk gram
黑暗 hāk ngam dark
黑色 hāk sīk black
口 háu mouth
口渴 háu hot thirsty
口譯員 háu yihk yùhn interpreter
喉嚨 hàuh lùhng throat
喉嚨痛 hàuh lùhng tung sore throat
候診室 hauh chán sāt waiting room
候機大堂 hauh gēi daaih tòhng terminal (airport)
後面 hauh mihn behind (direction)
起飛 héi fēi v leave
氣泵 hei bām air pump
汽車 hei chē car
汽車座位 hei chē joh wái car seat
氣喘 hei chyún asthmatic
戲劇 hei kehk n play (theater)
器皿 hei míhng utensil

汽船 hei syùhn motor boat
汽油 hei yàuh gasoline [petrol BE]
戲院 hei yún theater
靴 hēu boots
去 heui v go (somewhere)
香薰療法 hēung fān lìuh faat aromatherapy
香口膠 hēung háu gāau chewing gum
香水 hēung séui perfume
享用 héung yuhng v enjoy
顯示 hín sih v show
兄弟 hīng daih brother
可怕 hó pa terrible
河 hòh river
河谷 hòh gūk valley
學校 hohk haauh school
學習 hohk jaahp v study
學生 hohk sāang student
航班 hòhng bāan flight
航空公司 hòhng hūng gūng sī airline
航空信 hòhng hūng seun airmail
開 hōi turn on (lights)
開車 hōi chē v drive
開始 hōi chí v begin; start
開處方 hōi chyúh fōng v prescribe
開單 hōi dāan v bill (charge)
開罐器 hōi gun hei can opener

海關 **hói gwāan** customs

開酒器 **hōi jáu hei** corkscrew

開著 **hōi jeuhk** *adj* open

開瓶器 **hōi pìhng hei** bottle opener

開胃菜 **hōi waih choi** appetizer [starter BE]

海 **hói** sea

海灘 **hói tāan** beach

罕見 **hón gin** rare (object)

好 **hóu** *adj* good

好食 **hóu sihk** delicious

紅綠燈 **hùhng luhk dāng** traffic light

紅色 **hùhng sīk** red

胸圍 **hūng wàih** bra

血壓 **hyut ngaat** blood pressure

血液 **hyut yihk** blood

J

碴 **jā** carafe; jar

站 **jaahm** station

雜貨店 **jaahp fo dim** grocery store

雜誌 **jaahp ji** magazine

針灸 **jām gau** acupuncture

枕頭 **jám tàuh** pillow

真正 **jān jing** real

珍珠 **jān jyū** pearl

鎮 **jan** town

震驚 **jan gīng** stunning

質量 **jāt leuhng** quality

週末 **jāu muht** weekend

走 **jáu** *v* walk

酒吧 **jáu bā** bar (place)

酒店 **jáu dim** hotel

酒類表 **jáu leuih bíu** wine list

遮 **jē** umbrella

借記卡 **je gei kāat** debit card

最後 **jeui hauh** last

最好 **jeui hóu** best

嘴唇 **jéui sèuhn** lip

雀仔 **jeuk jái** bird

爵士樂 **jeuk sih ngohk** jazz

爵士樂俱樂部 **jeuk sih ngohk kēui lohk bouh** jazz club

准 **jéun** *v* permit

樽 **jēun** bottle

準備好 **jéun beih hóu** ready

准許 **jéun héui** *v* allow

進入 **jeun yahp** *v* enter

帳篷 **jeung fùhng** tent

帳篷杆 **jeung fùhng gōn** tent pole

帳蓬樁 **jeung fùhng jōng** tent peg

帳戶 **jeung wuh** account

支付 **jī fuh** *v* pay

支票 **jī piu** check [cheque BE]

支票戶口 **jī piu wuh háu** checking [current BE] account

紙 **jí** paper

紙幣 **jí baih** *n* bill (money)

指甲 **jí gaap** fingernail

趾甲 **jí gaap** toenail

指甲銼 **jí gaap cho** nail file

紙巾 **jí gān** paper towel; tissue

只係 **jí haih** only

止汗劑 **jí hon jāi** deodorant

姐妹 **jí múi** sister

指南 **jí nàahm** guide book

紫色 **jí sīk** purple

自動扶梯 **jih duhng fùh tāi** escalator

自動提款機 **jih duhng tàih fún gēi** ATM

自動提款卡 **jih duhng tàih fún kāat** ATM card

自助 **jih joh** self-service

寺廟 **jíh míu** temple (religious)

自然保護區 **jih yìhn bóu wuh kēui** nature preserve

直 **jihk** straight

植物園 **jihk maht yùhn** botanical garden

即棄 **jīk hei** disposable

即棄剃鬚刀 **jīk hei tai sōu dōu** disposable razor

即時訊息 **jīk sìh seun sīk** instant message

毯 **jīn** blanket

煎鍋 **jīn wō** frying pan

剪 **jín** trim (hair cut)

戰場 **jin chèuhng** battleground

戰爭紀念館 **jin jāng gei nihm gún** war memorial

蒸鍋 **jīng wō** steamer

證件 **jing gín** identification

症狀 **jing johng** condition (medical)

證明 **jing mìhng** certificate

證實 **jing saht** v confirm

接受 **jip sauh** v accept

折 **jit** discount

招待會 **jīu doih wúi** reception

左邊 **jó bīn** left (direction)

座位 **joh wái** seat

撞 **johng** v crash (car)

再見 **joi gin** goodbye

壯觀 **jong gūn** magnificent

租 **jōu** v rent

租用汽車 **jōu yuhng hei chē** rental [hire BE] car

早 **jóu** early

早餐 **jóu chāan** breakfast

祖父母 **jóu fuh móuh** grandparent

早晨 **jóu sàhn** good morning

做 **jouh** v have

做野 **jouh yéh** v work

足球 **jūk kàuh** soccer [football BE]

中午 **jūng bouh** noon

中等 **jūng dáng** medium (size)

中國 **jūng gwok** China

中國畫 jūng gwok wá Chinese painting

中文 jūng màhn Chinese

鍾意 jūng yi v like

腫 júng swelling

中暑 jung syú sunstroke

珠寶商 jyū bóu sēung jeweler

主菜 jyú choi main course

主要景點 jyú yiu gíng dím main attraction

住 jyuh v live

住喺 jyuh hái v stay

住宿 jyuh sūk accommodation

專家 jyūn gā specialist (doctor)

轉賬 jyún jeung v transfer (money)

轉 jyun v transfer (change trains/flights)

轉機 jyun gēi connection (flight)

轉角處 jyun gok chyu around (the corner)

鑽石 jyun sehk diamond

K

卡路里 kā louh léih calories

卡 kāat card

咭片 kāat pín business card

琴日 kàhm yaht yesterday

近 kahn close

吸塵器 kāp chàhn hei vacuum cleaner

咳 kāt n/v cough

購物 kau maht shopping

購物中心 kau maht jūng sām shopping centre [mall BE]

購物區 kau maht kēui shopping area

購物籃 kau maht láam basket (grocery store)

球拍 kàuh páak racket (sports)

期間 kèih gjāan during; period (of time)

奇怪 kèih gwaai strange

強姦 kèuhng gāan rape

區號 kēui houh area code

俱樂部 kēui lohk bouh club

區域 kēui wihk region

拒絕 kéuih jyuht v decline (credit card)

橋樑 kìuh lèuhng bridge

蓋印 koi yan v stamp (a ticket)

抗生素 kong sāng sou antibiotic

曲棍球 kūk gwan kàuh hockey

裙 kwàhn skirt

困難 kwan nàahn difficult

拳擊比賽 kyùhn gīk béi choi boxing match

L

肋骨 laahk gwāt rib (body part)

籃球 làahm kàuh basketball

藍色 làahm sīk blue

爛 **laahn** v break (tooth)

爛咗 **laahn jó** broken

冷 **láahng** cold (temperature)

冷氣 **láahng hei** air conditioning

垃圾 **laahp saap** garbage [rubbish BE]

垃圾袋 **laahp saap dói** garbage [rubbish BE] bag

辣 **laaht** hot (spicy)

拉 **lāai** v pull

攬 **láam** v hug

臨時 **làhm sìh** temporary

嚟 **làih** v come

禮拜 **láih baai** mass (church service)

禮品店 **láih bán dim** gift shop

禮服 **láih fuhk** dress (piece of clothing)

禮物 **láih maht** gift

褸 **lāu** jacket

流動性 **làuh dung sing** mobility

流行音樂 **làuh hàhng yām ngohk** pop music

流血 **làuh hyut** v bleed

樓梯 **làuh tāi** stairs

領呔 **léhng tāai** tie (clothing)

利 **leih** sharp

離婚 **lèih fān** v divorce

離開 **lèih hōi** departure

釐米 **lèih máih** centimeter

理髮師 **léih faat sī** barber

理解 **léih gáai** v understand

里數 **léih sou** mileage

靚 **leng** beautiful

輪椅 **lèuhn yí** wheelchair

輪椅道 **lèuhn yí douh** wheelchair ramp

涼 **lèuhng** cool (temperature)

量杯 **lèuhng būi** measuring cup

量羹 **lèuhng gāng** measuring spoon

涼鞋 **lèuhng hàaih** sandals

律師 **leuht sī** lawyer

雷雨 **lèuih yúh** thunderstorm

旅程 **léuih chìhng** trip

旅客 **léuih haak** tourist

旅行支票 **léuih hàhng jī piu** traveler's check [cheque BE]

旅行社 **léuih hàhng séh** travel agency

旅舍 **léuih se** hostel

旅遊資訊辦公室 **léuih yàuh jī seun baahn gūng sāt** tourist information office

連接 **lìhn jip** connection (internet); v connect (internet)

領事館 **líhng sih gún** consulate

令人驚奇嘅 **lihng yàhn gīng kèih ge** amazing

列印 **liht yan** v print

落 **lohk** v place (a bet)

落車 **lohk chē** get off (a train/ bus/subway)

樂趣 **lohk cheui** pleasure

浪漫 **lohng maahn** romantic

爐 **lòuh** stove

老 **lóuh** old

老公 **lóuh gūng** husband

老年人 **lóuh nìhn yàhn** senior citizen

老婆 **lóuh pòh** wife

路口位 **louh háu wái** aisle seat

路權 **louh kyùhn** right of way

路線 **louh sin** route

路線圖 **louh sin tòuh** road map

露營 **louh yìhng** v camp

露營爐 **louh yìhng lòuh** camping stove

綠色 **luhk sīk** green

聾 **lùhng** deaf

聯繫 **lyùhn haih** v contact

M

唔 **m** no

唔見咗 **m gin jó** v lose (something)

唔該 **m gōi** please

唔貴 **m gwai** inexpensive

晚餐 **máahn chāan** dinner

晚安 **máahn ngōn** good evening

慢慢地 **maahn máan déi** slowly

盲腸 **màahng chéung** appendix (body part)

買 **máaih** v buy

買野 **máaih yéh** v shop

賣 **maaih** v sell

賣花人 **maaih fā yàhn** florist

麻布 **màh bou** linen

麻醉 **màh jeui** anesthesia

媽媽 **màh mā** mother

民間音樂 **màhn gāan yām ngohk** folk music

文字 **màhn jih** n text (message)

敏感 **máhn gám** allergic

問題 **mahn tàih** problem; question

襪 **maht** sock

密碼 **maht máh** password

米黃色 **máih wòhng sīk** beige

蚊 **mān** Hong Kong currency

乜野 **māt yéh** what

微波爐 **mèih bō lòuh** microwave

美國 **méih gwok** United States (U.S.)

美國人 **méih gwok yàhn** American

美元 **méih yùhn** dollar (U.S.)

名 **méng** name

棉花 **mìhn fā** cotton

明信片 **mìhn seun pín** postcard

棉條 **mìhn tíu** tampon

面 **mihn** face

麵包舖 **mihn bāau póu** bakery

面部 **mihn bouh** facial

免費 **mín fai** free

免稅 **mín seui** duty-free

網吧 **móhng bā** internet cafe

網球 **móhng kàuh** tennis

剝 **mōk** v extract (tooth)

帽 **móu** hat

毛巾 **mòuh gān** towel

無限次使用嘅 **mòuh haahn chi sí yuhng ge** multiple-trip (ticket)

無酒精 **mòuh jáu jīng** non-alcoholic

無脂肪 **mòuh jī fōng** fat free

無聊嘅 **mòuh lìuh ge** boring

無味 **mòuh meih** bland

無線電話 **mòuh sin dihn wá** wireless phone

無線互聯網 **mòuh sin wuh lyùhn móhng** wireless internet

無線互聯網服務 **mòuh sin wuh lyùhn móhng fuhk mouh** wireless internet service

毛衣 **mòuh yī** sweater

無鉛 **mòuh yùhn** unleaded (gas)

冇 **móuh** without

舞蹈俱樂部 **móuh douh kēui lohk bouh** dance club

冇知覺 **móuh jī gok** unconscious

冇乜野 **móuh māt yéh** nothing

無人睇 **móuh yàhn tái** unattended

木炭 **muhk taan** charcoal

每 **múih** per

每個鐘頭 **múih go jūng tàuh** per hour

每個星期 **múih go sīng kèih** per week

每週 **múih jāu** weekly

每晚 **múih máahn** per night

每日 **múih yaht** per day

N

南 **nàahm** south

男仔 **nàahm jái** boy

男朋友 **nàahm pàhng yáuh** boyfriend

男人 **nàahm yán** man

難睇 **nàahn tái** ugly

奶粉 **náaih fán** formula (baby)

奶嘴 **náaih jéui** pacifier [soother BE]

奶樽 **náaih jēung** baby bottle

扭傷 **náu sēung** sprain

你好 **néih hóu** hello

女服務員 **néuih fuhk mouh yùhn** waitress

女仔 **néuih jái** girl

女裝恤衫 **néuih jōng sēut sāam** blouse

女朋友 **néuih pàhng yáuh** girlfriend

213

女人 néuih yán woman

顏色 ngàahn sīk color

眼 ngáahn eye

眼鏡 ngáahn géng glasses (optical)

硬幣 ngaahng beih coin

額外 ngaak ngoih extra

晏晝 ngaan jau noon [midday BE]

牙 ngàh tooth

牙膏 ngàh gōu toothpaste

牙醫 ngàh yī dentist

銀 ngàhn silver

銀包 ngàhn bāau purse; wallet

銀行 ngàhn hòhng bank

危險 ngàih hím dangerous

嘔 ngáu v vomit

牛仔布 ngàuh jái bou denim

牛仔褲 ngáuh jái fu jeans

午餐 ngh chāan lunch

午夜 ngh yeh midnight

餓 ngoh hungry

臥鋪車 ngoh pōu chē sleeper [sleeping BE] car

樂隊 ngohk déui orchestra

昂貴 ngòhng gwai expensive

愛 ngoi n/v love (someone)

愛爾蘭 ngoi yíh làahn Ireland

愛爾蘭人 ngoi yíh làahn yàhn Irish

外面 ngoih mihn outside

外套 ngoih tou coat

安全 ngōn chyùhn safe (protected)

安靜 ngōn jihng quiet

按 ngon v push

按摩 ngon mō massage

屋 ngūk house

呢 nī this

呢度 nī douh here

年 nìhn year

年輕 nìhn hīng young

年齡 nìhn nìhng age

尿 niuh urine

尿片 niuh pín diaper [nappy BE]

農產品 nùhng cháan bán produce

農產品商店 nùhng cháan bán sēung dim produce store

農場 nùhng chèuhng farm

暖 nyúhn adj/v warm

澳洲 ou jāu Australia

棒球 páahng kàuh baseball

排球賽 pàaih kàuh choi volleyball game

烹調 pāang tiùh v cook

跑馬場 páau máh chèuhng horse track

扒艇 pàh téhng rowboat

爬山電單車 **pàh sāan dihn dāan chē** mountain bike

貧血 **pàhn hyut** anemic

朋友 **pàhng yáuh** friend

噴髮劑 **pan faat jāi** hairspray

噴水池 **pan séui chìh** fountain

平 **pèhng** cheap

皮 **péi** leather

屁股 **pei gú** buttocks

皮帶 **pèih dáai** belt

皮膚 **pèih fū** skin

平底鑊 **pìhng dái wohk** saucepan

片 **pin** slice (of something)

票 **piu** ticket

膀胱 **pòhng gwōng** bladder

抱歉 **póu hip** sorry

普通 **póu tūng** regular

鋪位 **pou wái** berth

葡萄園 **pòuh tòuh yùhn** vineyard

配菜 **pui choi** side dish

S

沙漠 **sā mohk** desert

砂鍋 **sā wō** clay pot

曬傷 **saai sēung** sunburn

山 **sāan** mountain

刪除 **sāan chèuih** v delete

山頂 **sāan déng** peak (of a mountain)

山洞 **sāan duhng** cave

山仔 **sāan jái** hill

山路小徑 **sāan louh síu ging** trail

山路圖 **sāan louh tòuh** trail map

散紙 **sáan jí** change (money)

生日 **sāang yaht** birthday

殺蟲劑 **saat chùhng jāi** insect repellent

腎臟 **sahn johng** kidney (body part)

十字路口 **sahp jih louh háu** intersection

西部 **sāi bouh** west

西服套裝 **sāi fuhk tou jōng** suit

洗 **sái** v clean

洗潔精 **sái git jīng** dishwashing liquid

洗過嘅衫 **sái gwo ge sāam** laundry

洗頭水 **sái tàuh séui** shampoo

洗碗機 **sái wún gē** dishwasher

洗衣店 **sái yī dim** laundormat [launderette BE]

洗衣店設施 **sái yī dim chit sī** laundry facility

洗衣服務 **sái yī fuhk mouh** laundry service

洗衣機 **sái yī gēi** washing machine

細蚊仔 **sai mān jái** child

心口 **sām háu** chest (body part)

心口針 **sām háu jām** brooch

心口痛 **sām háu tung** chest pain

心臟 **sām johng** heart

心臟狀況 **sām johng johng fong** heart condition

森林 **sām làhm** forest

申報 **sān bou** *v* declare

新手 **sān sáu** novice (skill level)

新鮮 **sān sīn** fresh

失去 **sāt heui** lost

失物認領處 **sāt maht yihng líhng chyu** lost and found

失眠 **sāt mìhn** insomnia

室外游泳池 **sāt ngoih yàuh wihng chìh** outdoor pool

室內泳池 **sāt noih wihng chìh** indoor pool

膝頭 **sāt tàuh** knee

失業者 **sāt yihp jé** unemployed

修道院 **sāu douh yún** monastery

收費 **sāu fai** *n* charge (cost)

收據 **sāu geui** receipt

修腳趾甲 **sāu geuk jí gaap** pedicure

修理 **sāu léih** *v* fix (repair)

修手甲 **sāu sáu gaap** manicure

手 **sáu** hand

手臂 **sáu bei** arm

手錶 **sáu bīu** watch

手動汽車 **sáu duhng hei chē** manual car

手機 **sáu gēi** cell [mobile BE] phone

手掙 **sáu jāang** elbow

手指 **sáu jí** finger

手扼 **sáu ngáak** bracelet

首飾 **sáu sīk** jewelry

手提行李 **sáu tàih hàhng léih** carry-on [hand luggage BE]

手提箱 **sáu tàih sēung** suitcase

手推車 **sáu tēui chē** cart (grocery store)

手腕 **sáu wún** wrist

售票處 **sauh piu chyu** ticket office

寫 **sé** *v* write

錫 **sek** *v* kiss

醒 **séng** *v* wake

純銀 **sèuhn ngán** sterling silver

需要 **sēui yiu** *v* need

水池 **séui chìh** pool

水底呼吸設備 **séui dái fū kāp chit beih** snorkeling equipment

水晶 **séui jīng** crystal

睡袋 **seuih dói** sleeping bag

睡意 **seuih yi** drowsiness

睡衣 **seuih yī** pajamas

訊問處 **sēun mahn chyu** information desk

信封 **seun fūng** envelope

信件 **seun gín** letter

信息 **seun sīk** information (phone); message

信用卡 **seun yuhng kāat** credit card

箱 **sēung** box

商場 **sēung chèuhng** shopping mall [shopping centre BE]

雙程 **sēung chìhng** round-trip [return BE] (ticket)

商店目錄 **sēung dim muhk luhk** store directory

相反 **sēung fáan** opposite

傷口 **sēung háu** n cut (injury)

商務 **sēung mouh** business

商務艙 **sēung mouh chōng** business class

傷心 **sēung sām** sad

雙人床 **sēung yàhn chòhng** double bed

商業中心 **sēung yihp jūng sām** business center

相 **séung** photo

相機 **séung gēi** camera

相機套 **séung gēi tou** camera case

想嘔 **séung ngáu** nauseous

恤衫 **sēut sāam** shirt

絲綢 **sī chàuh** silk

CD **sī dī** CD

絲巾 **sī gīn** scarf

試吓 **si háh** v taste

絲襪 **sī maht** pantyhose

使用 **sí yuhng** v use

試身室 **si sān sāt** fitting room

市場 **síh chèuhng** market

市地圖 **síh deih tòuh** town map

時間 **sìh gaan** time

時間表 **sìh gaan bíu** schedule [timetable BE]

時裝店 **sìh jōng dim** clothing store

市政廳 **síh jing tēng** town hall

市中心 **síh jūng sām** downtown

市中心廣場 **síh jūng sām gwóng chèuhng** town square

食 **sihk** v eat

食物 **sihk maht** food

食藥 **sihk yeuhk** v take

食煙 **sihk yīn** v smoke; smoking (area)

城堡 **sìhng bóu** castle

乘客 **sìhng haak** passenger

舌 **siht** tongue

熄 **sīk** turn off (lights)

適合 **sīk hahp** fit (clothing)

線 **sin** line (train)

星期 **sīng kèih** week

攝氏 **sip sih** Celsius

攝影器材商店 **sip yínghei chòih sēung dim** camera store

燒 **sīu** v burn

消毒藥膏 **sīu duhk yeuk gōu** antiseptic cream

消防隊 **sīu fòhng yùhn** fire department

銷售稅 **sīu sauh seui** sales tax

小 **síu** small

小酒吧 **síu jáu bā** mini-bar

小組 **síu jóu** group

小溪 **síu kāi** stream

小路 **síu louh** trail [piste BE]

小路路線圖 **síu louh louh sin tòuh** trail [piste BE] map

小時 **síu sìh** hour

小食店 **síu sihk dim** snack bar

少少 **síu síu** little

梳 **sō** comb; hairbrush

炒鍋 **sō wō** wok

鎖 **só** n lock

鑰匙 **só sìh** key

鑰匙卡 **só sìh kāat** key card

鑰匙扣 **só sìh kau** key ring

桑拿 **sōng nàh** sauna

鬚後水 **sōu hauh séui** aftershave

帚把 **sou bá** broom

數字 **sou jih** number

數碼 **sou máh** digital

數碼相機 **sou máh séung gēi** digital camera

數碼相片 **sou máh seung pín** digital photo

數碼印刷品 **sou máh yan chaat bán** digital print

掃描器 **sou mìuh hei** scanner

素食者 **sou sihk jé** vegetarian

熟食 **suhk sihk** delicatessen

宿醉 **sūk jeui** hangover

宿舍 **sūk se** dormitory

送 **sung** v send

書 **syū** book

書店 **syū dim** bookstore

書法用品 **syū faat yuhng bán** calligraphy supplies

樹 **syuh** tree

船 **syùhn** boat

孫 **syūn** grandchild

損傷 **syún sēung** v damage

說唱樂 **syut cheung lohk** rap (music)

雪櫃 **syut gwaih** freezer

雪靴 **syut hēu** snowshoe

雪茄 **syut kā** cigar

T

太 **taai** too

太熟 **taai suhk** overdone

太陽 **taai yèuhng** sun

太陽眼鏡 **taai yèuhng ngáahn géng** sunglasses

探病時間 **taam behng sìh gaan** visiting hours

塔 **taap** tower

睇 **tái** v look

體操 tái chōu gym

睇見 tái gin *v* see

體育 tái yuhk sports

體育場 tái yuhk chèuhng stadium

體育用品商店 tái yuhk yuhng bán sēung dim sporting goods store

剃鬚刀 tai sōu dōu razor blade

剃鬚膏 tai sōu gōu shaving cream

吞 tān *v* swallow

偷 tāu *v* steal

偷竊 tāu sit theft

頭 tàuh head (body part)

頭等艙 tàuh dáng chōng first class

頭髮 tàuh faat hair

頭盔 tàuh kwāi helmet

投訴 tàuh sou complaint

頭痛 tàuh tung headache

頭暈眼花 tàuh wàhn ngáahn fā dizzy

推薦 tēui jin recommendation

腿 téui leg

退出 teui chēut *v* withdraw

退房 teui fóng check-out (hotel)

退休 teui yāu retired

T恤 tī sēut T-shirt

甜 tìhm sweet (taste)

填寫 tìhn sé *v* fill out (form)

停車 tìhng chē *v* park

停車場 tìhng chē chèuhng parking lot [car park BE]

停車計時器 tìhng chē gai sìh hei parking meter

停低 tìhng dāi *v* stop

天氣 tīn hei weather

聽日 tīng yaht tomorrow

聽力唔好 ting lihk m hóu hearing impaired

鐵軌 tit gwái track (train)

跳舞 tiu móuh *v* dance

拖車 tō chē tow truck

拖鞋 tō háai slippers

糖尿病 tòhng niuh behng diabetic

檯 tói table

托運 tok wahn *v* check (luggage)

湯羹 tōng gāng ceramic spoon

熨 tong *v* press (clothing)

熨斗 tong dáu *n* iron

熨衫 tong sāam *v* iron

肚屙 tóu ngō diarrhea

陶器 tòuh hei pottery

圖書館 tòuh syū gún library

同 tùhng with

銅 tùhng copper

同事 tùhng sih colleague

同一 tùhng yāt same

通知 tūng jī *v* notify

痛 tung pain

斷開 tyúhn hōi disconnect (computer)

還 **wàahn** *v* return

滑浪板 **waaht lohng báan** surfboard

滑水板 **waaht séui báan** water skis

壞咗 **waaih jó** damaged

玩 **wáan** *v* play

運動場 **wahn duhng chèuhng** field (sports)

運動鞋 **wahn duhng hàaih** sneaker

運動衫 **wahn duhng sāam** sweatshirt

暈浪 **wàhn lohng** travel sickness

運送 **wahn sung** *v* ship (mail)

餵 **wai** *v* feed

餵母乳 **wai móuh yúh** breastfeed

胃 **waih** stomach

為咗 **waih jó** for

衛生棉 **waih sāng mìhn** sanitary napkin [pad BE]

維生素 **wàih sāng sou** vitamin

胃痛 **waih tung** stomachache

溫泉 **wān chyùhn** hot spring

溫泉 **wān chyùhn** spa

V領 **wī léhng** V-neck

泳衣 **wihng yī** swimsuit

黃色 **wòhng sīk** yellow

污糟 **wū jōng** dirty

湖 **wùh** lake

護髮素 **wuh faat sou** conditioner

護照 **wuh jiu** passport

護照管制 **wuh jiu gún jai** passport control

互聯網 **wuh lyùhn móhng** internet

互聯網服務 **wuh lyùhn móhng fuhk mouh** internet service

護士 **wuh sih** nurse

換車 **wuhn chē** *v* change (buses)

換錢 **wuhn chín** *v* change (money)

換地方 **wuhn deih fōng** *v* exchange (place)

玩具店 **wuhn geui dim** toy store

玩具 **wuhn geuih** toy

換尿片 **wuhn niuh pín** *v* change (baby)

換現金 **wuhn yihn gām** *v* cash

回收 **wùih sāu** recycling

會係 **wúih haih** *v* be

會員證 **wúih yùhn jing** membership card

會議 **wuih yíh** conference; meeting

會議室 **wuih yíh sāt** meeting room

會議廳 **wuih yíh tēng** convention hall

碗 **wún** bowl

任何野 **yahm hòh yéh** anything

人民幣 **yàhn màhn baih** Ren Min Bi (Chinese currency)

入場 **yahp chèuhng** admission

入口 **yahp háu** entrance

日 **yaht** day

日期 **yaht kèih** date (calendar)

陰道 **yām douh** vagina

陰道傳染 **yām douh chyùhn yíhm** vaginal infection

陰莖 **yām ging** penis

音樂 **yām ngohk** music

音樂商店 **yām ngohk sēung dim** music store

音樂廳 **yām ngohk tēng** concert hall

音樂會 **yām ngohk wúi** concert

飲 **yám** v drink

飲料 **yám liuh** n drink

飲料單 **yám liuh dāan** drink menu

飲用水 **yám yuhng séui** drinking water

隱形眼鏡 **yán yìhng ngáahn géng** contact lens

隱形眼鏡液 **yán yìhng ngáahn géng yihk** contact lens solution

一打 **yāt dā** dozen

一共 **yāt guhng** total (amount)

一樓 **yāt láu** ground floor

休息得好好 **yāu sīk dāk hóu hóu** well-rested

休息室 **yāu sīk sāt** restroom [toilet BE]

油 **yàuh** oil

遊蕩者 **yàuh dong jé** loafers

郵寄 **yàuh gei** v mail

郵件 **yàuh gín** n mail [post BE]

郵局 **yàuh gúk** post office

遊戲 **yàuh hei** game

遊戲圍欄 **yàuh hei wàih làahn** playpen

遊覽 **yàuh láahm** excursion; tour

遊覽勝地 **yàuh láahm sing deih** attraction (place)

遊樂園 **yàuh lohk yùhn** amusement park

郵票 **yàuh piu** n stamp (postage)

游水 **yàuh séui** v swim

郵箱 **yàuh sēung** mailbox [postbox BE]

猶太教堂 **yàuh taai gaau tóng** synagogue

猶太食品 **yàuh taai sihk bán** kosher

有趣 **yáuh cheui** interesting

有空房 **yáuh hūng fóng** vacancy

有咗 **yáuh jó** pregnant

有早餐嘅酒店 **yáuh jóu chāan ge jáu dim** bed and breakfast

有吸引力嘅 **yáuh kāp yáhn lihk** attractive

有遠見 **yáuh yúhn gin** far-sighted [long-sighted BE]

野餐區 **yéh chāan kēui** picnic area

夜 **yeh** night

夜總會 **yeh júng wúi** nightclub

夜晚 **yeh máahn** evening

藥房 **yeuhk fòhng** pharmacy [chemist BE]

藥方 **yeuhk fōng** prescription

藥膏 **yeuhk gōu** cream (ointment)

弱視者 **yeuhk sih jé** visually impaired

藥丸 **yeuhk yún** tablet (medicine)

羊毛 **yèuhng mòuh** wool

氧氣治療 **yéuhng hei jih liuh** oxygen treatment

約 **yeuk** appointment

衣物 **yī maht** clothing

衣物櫃 **yī maht gwaih** locker

醫生 **yī sāng** doctor

醫藥 **yī yeuhk** medicine

醫院 **yī yún** hospital

意外 **yi ngoih** accident

以前 **yíh chìhn** before

胰島素 **yìh dóu sou** insulin

兒科醫生 **yìh fō yī sāng** pediatrician

兒童菜單 **yìh tùhng choi dāan** children's menu

兒童飯量 **yìh tùhng faahn leuhng** children's portion

兒童泳池 **yìh tùhng wihng chìh** kiddlie [paddling BE] pool

宜家 **yìh gā** now

以後 **yíh hauh** after; later

耳仔 **yíh jái** ear

耳仔痛 **yíh jái tung** earache

耳筒 **yíh túng** headphones

耳環 **yíh wáan** earrings

嚴肅 **yìhm sūk** serious

驗光師 **yìhm gwōng sī** optician

現金 **yìhn gām** *n* cash

營地 **yìhng deih** campsite

研討會 **yìhng tóu wúi** seminar

營業時間 **yìhng yihp sìh gaan** business hours

熱 **yiht** hot (temperature)

煙 **yīn** cigarette

煙草零售商 **yīn chóu lìhng sauh sēung** tobacconist

英鎊 **yīng bóng** pound (British sterling)

英國 **yīng gwok** United Kingdom (U.K.)

英國人 **yīng gwok yàhn** British

英文 **yīng màhn** English

嬰兒紙巾 **yīng yìh jí gān** baby wipe

影相 **yíng séung** photography

影印本 **yíng yan bún** photocopy

要塞 **yiu choi** fort

搖籃 **yìuh láam** crib

娛樂 **yùh lohk** entertainment

雨 **yúh** rain

乳房 **yúh fòhng** breast

雨林 **yúh làhm** rainforest

雨褸 **yúh lāu** raincoat

乳糖過敏 **yúh tòhng gwo máhn** lactose intolerant

預報 **yuh bou** forecast

預定 **yuh dihng** reservation; v reserve

預定日程 **yuh dihng yaht chìhng** v schedule

愉快 **yuh faai** happy

預支現金 **yuh jī yìhn gām** cash advance

遠 **yúhn** far

圓領 **yùhn léhng** crew neck

原諒 **yùhn leuhng** v excuse

懸崖 **yùhn ngàaih** cliff

容易 **yùhng yih** easy

用 **yuhng** v cost

用盡 **yuhng jeuhn** exhausted

用信用卡畀錢 **yuhng seun yuhng kāat béi chín** v charge (credit card)

用戶名 **yuhng wuh méng** username

月 **yuht** month

月經 **yuht gīng** period (menstrual)

月臺 **yuht tòih** platform

玉 **yúk** jade